PRACTICAL VOCABULARY

Second Edition

NEW YORK

Library of Congress Cataloging-in-Publication Data:
    Practical vocabulary—2nd ed.
        p.cm.
    ISBN 10 1-57685-567-8
    ISBN 13 978-1-57685-567-6
    1. Vocabulary problems—exercises, etc. I. Learning Express (Organization)
PE1449.M428 2006
428.1—dc22

                                                            2006046510

Printed in the United States of America

9 8 7 6 5 4 3 2 1

Second Edition

ISBN 10: 1-57685-567-8
ISBN 13: 978-1-57685-567-6

For information on LearningExpress, other LearningExpress products, or bulk sales,
please call or write to us at:
        LearningExpress
        55 Broadway
        8th Floor
        New York, NY 10006

Visit us at:
        www.learnatest.com

CONTENTS

Introduction: *An Invitation*   v

Pretest   1

1 Words from Law, Politics, and Current Events   5

2 Word Meaning from Sight   17

3 Words from Literature, the Arts, and Popular Culture   27

4 Word Meaning from Sound   37

5 Words from Science and Technology   49

6 Word Meaning from Structure   59

7 Words from Medicine and Healthcare   67

8 Word Meaning from Roots   75

9 Words from Business and Finance   83

10 Word Meaning from Prefixes   93

11 Words from Names   103

12 Word Meaning from Suffixes   115

13 Words from Other Lands and Languages   125

14 Word Meaning from Context   135

15 Words from Computer Technology   145

16 Idioms and Vocabulary Variations   155

17 New and Emerging Vocabulary   165

18 Campus-Speak   175

19 Looking Backward   183

20 Looking Forward   197

Posttest   207

Appendix: *Master Word List*   211

INTRODUCTION
An Invitation

So much to learn, so little time. The demands of school, jobs, family, and community can seem overwhelming at times. Every day, there are exciting things going on and new ideas taking shape that will change the way you look at who you are and what you do. You experience many of these events and ideas visually—what you read in newspapers, magazines, and books, on signs, and even on the computer screen. Others you discover through sound—on radio or TV, in films and conversations. To be able to share in and be part of this incredible process of communication, you have to have access to its common currency—the language that expresses the ideas, gives the instructions, and reports the events that unite us as a society.

This book is an invitation. It's an invitation to take a break from each busy day, to attend an important daily meeting—a meeting with words. By doing one lesson a day, you'll discover the keys to unlocking the meaning of hundreds, perhaps thousands, of words unfamiliar to you now. By taking these new words and adding them to your own language store, you'll increase your ability to express your own ideas and experiences to other people and to better understand other people's ideas in what you read and hear around you. Most importantly, you will gain greater insight into the English language and will develop valuable strategies for learning new words easily and quite naturally as you live your life, busy as it is.

HOW TO USE THIS BOOK

Begin by answering the list of questions in the self-assessment exercise that follows. It will help you assess what you already know about the English language and what you need to do to have a larger, more usable English vocabulary.

A Little a Day

Choose a time each day that you set aside just for you. Think about when would be the best time for you. It may be early in the morning with your first cup of coffee. It might be at noon with your lunch or on a work break when you can be alone. For some, working on this book may be the winding-down activity that comes right before going to bed. Or perhaps it can be part of your commute to work or school. Whenever the time is right, just make sure you do it regularly—at least five days a week for a month.

Practice Really Listening

Use audiotapes. English is a difficult language to learn because it is so visually confusing. You'll see how to address that problem later, but for now, just remember that one of the ways you most often encounter vocabulary is by listening. Vocabulary tapes and CDs are available in libraries and bookstores. You may also find it helpful to record the new words in this book yourself on a CD at home.

Immerse Yourself in Words

Get into the habit of *noticing* words all the time. Carry a small notebook with you and jot down interesting words as you meet them in your daily life. Don't know how to spell a word you hear? It doesn't matter; write it down just as it sounds to you and look it up later.

If You Own It, Live in It!

As you work your way through this book, select the words you particularly want to add to your personal store of usable vocabulary. Write them on the inside back cover of this book. (If you have borrowed this book from a library or a friend, do the exercises and keep the list in a separate notebook.) If the book belongs to you, live in it. Write in the margins. Settle in for a month and walk around its pages. By the end of the four weeks, you should feel as if you've always lived there, but the "furniture"—the words you have learned—will have taken up permanent residence in your head.

Share the Work—and the Wealth!

Because you learn best when you use all your senses, you will learn these words more quickly if you have a "study buddy" to quiz you on new words. And by working together, you'll both learn new words and discover the strategies for approaching unfamiliar words and terms.

And Finally . . . Enjoy!

Joining the company of the "word-ly wise" doesn't have to be hard work. It mostly takes curiosity. Jump on those unfamiliar words that pop up in conversation or in reading. Take them apart. Welcome them to your world. Share them with a friend. You'll be greatly rewarded for your efforts—because long after this book is back at the library or on your bookshelf, you'll find you've got a lifetime of pleasure in words ahead of you.

SELF-ASSESSMENT QUESTIONS

Put a check mark next to the sentences that describe your own vocabulary habits.

_____**1.** I don't feel confident that I express myself well when I speak.

_____**2.** I sometimes feel uncomfortable when I know what I want to say but just can't think of the right word.

_____**3.** I notice unfamiliar words in print and feel that I should know them.

_____**4.** I have trouble remembering words I learned in school.

_____**5.** If I write down new words, I remember them better.

_____**6.** Sometimes, I notice that words look and sound like other words.

_____**7.** If I come across an unfamiliar word in print, I usually look it up in the dictionary.

_____**8.** If I come across an unfamiliar word in print, I usually ask someone what it means.

_____**9.** If I hear an unfamiliar word in conversation or on the radio or TV, I usually ask someone what it means.

_____**10.** If I meet a word I don't know, I'm usually too embarrassed to ask for help or to look up its meaning.

The answers to these questions should give you a sense of how you feel about your present approach to learning new vocabulary. The purpose of this book is to help you find new ways of approaching and improving that search.

GETTING TO KNOW AND USE WORDS

Before we look at the first set of vocabulary words, here are a few ideas you should keep in mind.

Read, Speak, Listen

Everyone has three vocabularies in every language he or she speaks: a *reading vocabulary*, a *speaking vocabulary*, and a *listening vocabulary*. You've read words you have never heard, and heard words you've never read. Your speaking vocabulary may ignore many words you have either read or heard but do not use. As you explore the vocabulary in this book, think about bringing these three large sets of words together into a rich and useful database that will serve you well.

The Four Approaches

As you continue in this book, you'll be working with four specific approaches to looking at unfamiliar words and understanding their meaning. For example, what happens when you first meet a new word?

Ask yourself:

 Sight: **Does it look like anything I've ever seen?**

 Sound: **Does it sound like anything I've ever heard?**

 Structure: **Is there any part of it—like a word root, a prefix, or a suffix—that seems familiar?**

 Context: **How does the "frame" of the sentence help determine word meaning?**

These four symbols will appear next to selected words throughout the book. They're there to remind you of the four approaches to recognizing unfamiliar words. You'll see examples of some of the symbols used in the Answers section at the end of each lesson.

Not everyone "sees" words in the same way. You might, for example, respond to a visual clue in a word, or you might instead hear a familiar sound in that word. Another person reading that same word might recognize a structural clue in the word; for instance, she might grasp its meaning by associating the word's prefix with that same prefix on another word she knows. The bottom line is that since you can't be sure which strategy will work for you when, try them all!

Sound It Out

When you come upon a new word in your reading, how do you know how to pronounce it? You sound it out, using *phonetics*—the study of how letter combinations and words sound. You'll find out more about phonetics later in the book, but for now, take a look at the following simplified phonetic spelling system. This system will be used throughout this book. You may want to photocopy this page so you will be able to refer to it easily.

a as in c**a**t

ah as in traum**a**

ahr as in c**ar**

ay as in g**a**te

e as in **e**gg

ee as in s**ee**n

i as in d**i**d

eye (or sometimes just *y*)
    as in d**ie**

oo as in m**oo**n

oh as in s**o**fa

ore as in m**ore**

oy as in b**oy** or f**oi**l

ow as in c**ow**

u as in f**u**n

yoo as in c**u**te

uh as in ag**e**nt (known as
    the *scwha* sound)

ur as in cent**er**

k as in **c**old

s as in **c**enter

j as in **g**ym

g as in **g**um

th as in **th**at

th as in **th**ink

ks as in e**x**pect

zh as in a**z**ure or mea**s**ure

PRETEST

Before you start your vocabulary study, you may want to get an idea of how much you already know and how much you need to learn. The pretest consists of two or three words from each of the lessons, and you must match words in column A with their definitions in column B. Naturally, 40 questions can't cover every single concept, idea, or shortcut you will learn by working through this book. So even if you identify all the words on the pretest correctly, it's almost guaranteed that you will find a few concepts or tricks in this book that you didn't already know. On the other hand, if you get a lot of the answers wrong on this pretest, don't despair. This book will show you how to increase your vocabulary, step by step.

PRACTICAL VOCABULARY

Match each word in column A with its definition in column B.

A

1. triage *e*

2. laugh off *u*

3. acquittal *n*

4. pseudonym *s*

5. malady *x*

6. subsidize *c*

7. eschew *m*

8. micromanage *t*

9. barrio *j*

10. fiasco *√*

11. malapropism *g*

12. incentive *q*

13. transcript *bb*

14. coterie *ee*

15. upload *z*

16. narcissistic *kk*

17. executor *dd*

18. soliloquy *b*

19. dormant

20. hiatus

21. monopoly

22. surrogate

23. cameo

B

a. to make faster or simpler

b. a speech given by a single speaker

c. a substitute or replacement, or one who is a legal sponsor for a child; in legal usage, a surrogate court is one that deals with custody and/or adoption issues

d. mutually dependant

e. the process by which the most severely injured are singled out for prompt treatment (originally performed by separating the injured according to three orders of priority)

f. excited attention that builds with public awareness of a problem

g. a humorous misuse of the language

h. close communication between people

i. weakened

j. a Spanish-speaking area in a city

k. be careful

l. a surgical cut

m. avoid

n. the act of finding a defendant not guilty in a court of law

o. the settling of disputes by a third party who has no stake in either side

p. to support financially a group or institution that cannot manage independently

q. a shortening of perquisite, which means a benefit of employment

r. a leave permitted by teachers to pursue advanced study, travel, or opportunities for professional development

s. a false name used to disguise identity

t. to closely supervise the management of the daily operations of workers in the company

2

24. holistic

25. furor

26. expedite

27. rhinestone

28. watch out

29. voicemail

30. rapport

31. draconian

32. sabbatical

33. perk

34. symbiotic

35. incision

36. cartel

37. debilitated

38. arbitration

39. etiology

40. utopian

u. ignore with good humor

v. a complete failure

w. harsh and punitive

x. a condition of illness; an ailment

y. a period of time between activities; an interval

z. to transfer (data or programs), usually from a peripheral computer or device to a central, often remote computer

aa. the union of a group of businesses that have joined together for the purpose of controlling an industry

bb. an official copy of a student's school record

cc. the medical practice that concerns itself with the whole person—physically, psychologically, and emotionally

dd. one who represents the interests of a client's estate

ee. a close group of friends or supporters; an entourage

ff. encouragement

gg. control of a market by a single business

hh. a system or device that answers the telephone and records messages

ii. a colorless artificial gem of paste or glass

jj. at rest or inactive

kk. one who is self-absorbed and conceited

ll. a brief, often uncredited role in a movie or television program; it can also mean a style of jewelry in which a stone appears with one image carved on top of another

mm. describing an ideal society

nn. the study of the origin or cause of illness

ANSWERS

1. e (Lesson 7)

2. u (Lesson 16)

3. n (Lesson 2)

4. s (Lesson 3)

5. x (Lesson 8)

6. p (Lesson 10)

7. m (Lesson 20)

8. t (Lesson 17)

9. j (Lesson 13)

10. v (Lesson 13)

11. g (Lesson 11)

12. ff (Lesson 20)

13. bb (Lesson 18)

14. ee (Lesson 14)

15. z (Lesson 15)

16. kk (Lesson 12)

17. dd (Lesson 2)

18. b (Lesson 3)

19. jj (Lesson 6)

20. y (Lesson 4)

21. gg (Lesson 10)

22. c (Lesson 5)

23. ll (Lesson 4)

24. cc (Lesson 5)

25. f (Lesson 1)

26. a (Lesson 1)

27. ii (Lesson 11)

28. k (Lesson 16)

29. hh (Lesson 15)

30. h (Lesson 14)

31. w (Lesson 12)

32. r (Lesson 18)

33. q (Lesson 17)

34. d (Lesson 6)

35. l (Lesson 8)

36. aa (Lesson 9)

37. i (Lesson 7)

38. o (Lesson 9)

39. nn (Lesson 7)

40. mm (Lesson 12)

1

WORDS FROM LAW, POLITICS, AND CURRENT EVENTS

In this lesson, you will encounter new words from the areas of law, politics, and current events. You will notice the appearance, the sound, and the structure of those words and think about how each one is used in a sentence. This will set the stage for a review of word recognition skills in the next several lessons.

What happens when you first come across a new word? Maybe you're used to just skipping over it. But you won't learn anything that way! If you're serious about building your vocabulary, your best resource is new words that you encounter in print or in spoken language, as in conversations or on the radio or television. When you find a new word, write it down, using a phonetic spelling if you aren't sure of the correct spelling. Before you go to the dictionary, see what you can find out about the word using the four approaches outlined in the introduction.

- **Sight:** Does the word look like another word I've seen before?
- **Sound:** Does the word sound like anything I've heard before?
- **Structure:** Is there any part of the word that looks familiar?
- **Context:** If I take the word out of the sentence, can I put another word in its place and keep the same meaning?

HOW TO USE THE WORD LISTS

You're about to tackle your first Word List. Each lesson of this book will give you a new Word List. First, you'll be given sentences that put each word in context, with some instructions about what to do with those sentences. The Word List words will be in bold type. Also, some words will have a special symbol in front of them; these symbols are shown on page viii of the Introduction. The symbols show a good approach to guessing the meaning of the word. The explanation of how to use this approach for the given word appears in the Answers section at the end of each lesson.

After the Word List in most lessons, there will be a table for you to fill in, based on what you know or can figure out—about that lesson's words, using the sight, sound, structure, and context strategies. That table appears again, with the blanks filled in, in the Answers section at the end of the lesson.

After the table, you complete the A Closer Look section, again using sight, sound, structure, and context for further help in finding meanings. After that is a list that gives the meaning and phonetic pronunciation of each word. You can compare that list to the sentences to help see how each word functions in context. Then, knowing the meaning of each word, you complete Practice Exercises that will help you solidify them in your memory. Answers to A Closer Look and Practice Exercises appear at the end of the lesson after the filled-in table.

WORD LIST 1

What follows are the sentences that contain the words for your first Word List. The Word List words are in bold. Here's what to do:

- Read all the sentences.
- Underline words in bold you already know and can define on sight.
- Put a star over words in bold that seem familiar but that you cannot define on sight.
- Circle words in bold that are unfamiliar to you.

Sentences

Israeli **realists** must defend the prime minister's foreign policy against the objections of **hardliners** within the government.

A **bipartisan coalition** in Congress could **expedite** flood relief in the Midwest and thus allow aid to be sent more quickly to the stricken area.

bipartisan

The legislature is considering a proposal that would permit welfare **recipients** to receive **vouchers** for needed supplies rather than checks for cash.

voucher

Incumbent lawmakers usually have an advantage over less **seasoned** candidates in a close election.

seasoned

The president of the United States can **veto** legislative bills, which makes them inactive.

Sometime, when a **defendant** loses a lawsuit, he or she has to pay **punitive** damages to the plaintiff.

As a result of the **furor** surrounding charges of **harassment** in the military and policies regarding **fraternization** between ranks, some have called for a review of the sexual politics of the armed services.

Now look at the 15 boldfaced words in the sentences you just read. Fill in the information on the table that follows, based only on what you know or can guess about the word. The first few words have been filled in for you to show you how it's done. You fill in the ones that have been left blank.

Word List 1: Practice Table

Word	Sight: Does it look familiar?	Sound: It sounds like . . .	Structure: Part of it reminds me of . . .	Context: It is used to mean . . .
realists	not much help here	REE-uhl-lists	-*ist* usually means "one who"	"against the protest of the hardliners" sounds like someone who is more flexible
hardliners	looks like someone who is pretty rigid in his views	hahrd-LYEN-urz	no mysteries here	pretty obvious
bipartisan	party, maybe political parties	bye-PAHR-ti-zan	*bi-* usually means two	a two-party system?
coalition	looks like coal, but that doesn't make sense here	koh-a-LISH-un	*co-* usually means "together"	something that works together?
expedite				
recipient				
voucher				

Word	Sight: Does it look familiar?	Sound: It sounds like . . .	Structure: Part of it reminds me of . . .	Context: It is used to mean . . .
incumbent				
seasoned				
veto				
defendant				
punititve				
furor				
harassment				
fraternization				

A CLOSER LOOK
How Words Look

In the next lesson, you will learn how to recognize words by sight. Start now to pay attention to the look of the words you meet.

What other words would you recognize as related to the following words?

1. bipartisan   party, _____

2. fraternization   fraternity, _____

3. veto   vote, _____

4. defendant   defend, _____

5. seasoned   .   season, _____

How Words Are Spelled

Fill in the missing letters to spell each word correctly.

6. pun__ __ __ ve

7. fur__ __

8. ex__ __ __ite

9. rec__ __ient

10. ha__ __ssment

Meanings for Word List 1

Here are the words from this lesson with their pronunciations and meanings. See how many you came close to figuring out.

realist (REE-uhl-ist): someone inclined to the literal truth and pragmatism

hardliner (hahrd-LYEN-ur): someone who has strong opinions about government (or other) policies

bipartisan (bye-PAHR-ti-zuhn): between two political parties

coalition (koh-uh-LI-shun): a joining of two or more parties or groups in a common cause

expedite (ECKS-puh-dyte): to make faster or simpler

recipient (ree-SIP-ee-uhnt): one who receives something

voucher (VOW-chur): written permit to receive goods or services instead of cash

incumbent (in-KUM-buhnt): one who is currently serving in a political office

seasoned (SEE-zund): experienced, as in a seasoned baseball pitcher. It can also mean "flavored," as in a highly seasoned dish

veto (VEE-toe): to prevent a legislative bill from becoming law by rejecting it

punitive (PYOO-nuh-tiv): inflicting or aiming to inflict punishment; punishing

defendant (dee-FEN-duhnt): the party against which an action is brought in a court of law

furor (FYOOR-or): excited attention that builds with public awareness of a problem

harassment (HAIR-ass-ment or huh-RASS-muhnt): subjecting someone to unpleasantness or unwanted attention, often in an effort to gain power or control over that person

fraternization (frat-ur-neye-ZAY-shun): forbidden relationships in the military—with enemy soldiers or among ranks, particularly between men and women of different ranks. In its literal sense, it means "friendly or brotherly behavior"

PRACTICE EXERCISES

Test your memory of the words in this lesson.

Fill in the Blanks

Choose from Word List 1 to complete each of the following sentences.

11. _____ players help rookies learn how to handle the pressure of stardom in sports.

12. Some parents want a _____ system that will allow them to send their children to a school of their choice.

13. She was the _____ of a check worth thousands of dollars!

14. The president _____ the bill on prohibiting drilling in the Arctic Wildlife Refuge.

15. The _____ got caught in a lie while taking the stand and was subsequently found guilty by the jury.

Yes or No?

Answer the following questions with Yes or No, depending on the meaning of the italicized words.

16. _____Would a *hardliner* be difficult during negotiations?

17. _____Is *fraternization* encouraged by the military?

18. _____Are most *realists* considered dreamy idealists?

19. _____Do you pay *punitive* damages if you are injured in a car accident?

20. _____Would a *coalition* bring together like-minded people?

ANSWERS

Here are some ways you could use the four approaches for some of the words in Word List 1.

Bipartisan has structure clues in the prefix *bi-*, which means "two," and in the word *partisan*, which means "having to do with a political party."

Voucher has a sound clue in the word *vouch*, which means "to speak for."

Seasoned looks like the familiar word *season*, a part of the year.

On the following pages are some suggested answers for the questions posed in the table about Word List 1. Your answers may be different, but this table shows some of the most helpful clues.

Word List 1: Answer Table

Word	Sight: Does it look familiar?	Sound: It sounds like . . .	Structure: Part of it reminds me of . . .	Context: It is used to mean . . .
realists	not much help here	REE-uhl-lists	*-ist* usually means "one who"	"against the protest of the hardliners" sounds like someone who is more flexible
hardliners	looks like someone who is pretty rigid in his views	hahrd-LYEN-urz	no mysteries here	pretty obvious
bipartisan	party, maybe political parties	bye-PAHR-ti-zan	*bi-* usually means two	a two-party system?
coalition	looks like coal, but that doesn't make sense here	koh-a-LISH-un	*co-* usually means "together"	something that works together?
expedite	no help here	ECKS-puh-dite	*ex-* usually means "out of" or "away from"	The work *quickly* suggests that *expedite* means "speed up."
recipient	*receive* (not recipe!)	ree-SIP-ee-uhnt	*-ent* usually signals a noun	If they "recieve vouchers," then *recipient* is "one who recieves."
voucher	*vouch*	VOW-chur	*-er* usually means "one who," but that doesn't make sense here	Contrast with "checks for cash" suggests something you can use instead of cash

Word	Sight: Does it look familiar?	Sound: It sounds like . . .	Structure: Part of it reminds me of . . .	Context: It is used to mean . . .
incumbent	no help	in-KUM-bent	*-ent* usually signals a noun	Contrast with "less seasoned" suggests someone experienced
seasoned	*season*	SEE-zund	no help	Suggests experience
veto	*vote*	VEE-toe	no help here	The sentence states that when the president vetoes a bill, he makes it inactive; therefore, *veto* must mean to reject.
defendant	*defend*	DEE-fend-duhnt	no help here	Because a *defendant* has to pay damages if he or she loses a lawsuit, the word probably means "someone who is sued" or "acted against."
punititve	*punish*	PYOO-nuh-tiv	no help here	*Punitive* sounds like "punish," so to pay *punitive* damages probably means to pay damages that are meant to punish the offender.

Word	Sight: Does it look familiar?	Sound: It sounds like . . .	Structure: Part of it reminds me of . . .	Context: It is used to mean . . .
furor	looks like *fury*	FYOOR-or	no help here	"Charges" and "call for review" suggests some kind of fuss.
harassment	*harass*	HAIR-ass-muhnt *or* ha-RASS-muhnt	*-ment* usually signals a noun	"Charges" probably indicates something illegal
fraternization	*fraternity*	frat-er-neye-ZAY-shun	*-tion* usually signals a noun	"Between the ranks" and needing a "policy" suggests something bad—bad brotherly relationships?

A Closer Look

How Words Look

1. bicycle (or any other bi- word)
2. fraternal
3. voter
4. defense
5. seasoning

How Words Are Spelled

6. pun*iti*ve
7. fur*or*
8. ex*ped*ite
9. re*ci*pient
10. ha*ra*ssment

Practice Exercises

Fill in the Blanks

11. seasoned
12. voucher
13. recipient
14. vetoed
15. defendant

Yes or No?

16. Yes
17. No
18. No
19. No
20. Yes

IN SHORT

In this lesson, you met some words drawn from the kinds of reading materials you might encounter every day, or topics you might hear about in the news. In addition, you had a chance to consider how you might approach unfamiliar words. In the next lesson, you will consider one of the approaches that helps uncover word meaning: knowing words by how they look.

WORD MEANING FROM SIGHT

In the next few lessons, you will revisit the four approaches to word meaning and learn how to use each one to recognize new words. Before encountering entirely new words in this lesson, you'll first return to words from Lesson 1 to review the first approach: recognizing words by sight. You will notice how some words look familiar right away because you see familiar features in them.

The English language is particularly difficult to read because in addition to the many different sound combinations that carry their own exceptions and oddities, many words are also visually confusing. Here are some things to keep in mind when you recognize a word that you encounter but are still unsure of its meaning.

RECOGNIZING WORDS BY THEIR LOOKS

In Word List 1, you saw a number of words that are near relatives to other words. They are a little like distant cousins; they share some family characteristics but are not in the immediate family.

- **Vouchers** suggests the word *vouch*, meaning "to speak for."
- **Veto** is a near relation to *vote*.
- **Fraternization** brings to mind *fraternity*.

RECOGNIZING WORDS BY HOW THEY WORK IN SENTENCES

When you are unsure of the meaning of a word, you may be helped by noting how the word works in its sentence—its part of speech. At the very least, recognizing the part of speech will help you rule out some meanings that might otherwise occur to you. When you saw the word *expedite* in one of the sentences from Lesson 1, it may have reminded you of the word *expedition*, which means "a trip" or "journey." But then, when you looked at the sentence, you could see that the word *expedite* was used as a verb (an action word). Since *expedition* is a noun (or a word that names a thing), you could therefore conclude that *expedite* could not mean "a trip."

The parts of speech that help us recognize vocabulary words are:

- **noun** (*n*)—names a person, place, or thing
- **verb** (*v*)—tells of action or being
- **adjective** (*adj*)—describes a noun or pronoun
- **adverb** (*adv*)—describes a verb, an adjective, or other adverb

Practice identifying the parts of speech of the italicized words by looking again at this sentence from Lesson 1:

A *bipartisan coalition* in Congress could *expedite* flood relief in the Midwest and thus allow aid to be sent more *quickly* to the stricken area.

Here are these words with their parts of speech:

- *Bipartisan* is an **adjective** that describes the noun *coalition*.
- *Coalition* is a **noun** that names a specific thing, an *alliance*.
- *Expedite* is a **verb** that tells the action of speeding up assistance.
- *Quickly* is an **adverb** describing the verb *sent*.

In the following sentence, also taken from Lesson 1, three of the nouns are italicized. Can you find two adjectives in the sentence?

> Israeli *realists* must defend the prime minister's foreign policy against the objections of *hardliners* in the government.

Remember, adjectives describe nouns: Thus, *foreign* clarifies "what kind of" policy is being discussed, and *Israeli* tells more information about the realists involved in the debate.

In the following sentence from Lesson 1, circle the verbs:

> The legislature is considering a proposal that would permit welfare recipients to receive vouchers for needed supplies rather than checks for cash.

You should have circled *is considering*, *would permit*, and *receive*.

RECOGNIZING WORDS THAT LOOK LIKE OTHERS

Words that look alike but that sound and mean different things are *homographs*. Notice that the different sound in these words can come from the accent, or stress, on one part of the word. For example, *conduct* has two distinct meanings and pronunciations:

> kun-DUKT (*v*) means "to lead" or "direct." Sample sentence: "I will *conduct* the orchestra for the last song."
> KON-dukt (*n*) means "behavior." Sample sentence: "His *conduct* in school was terrible."

Another thing to watch for are words that sound the same and may look *alike* as well but mean different things. They are called *homonyms*. For example, *season* has several meanings:

> a part of the year (*n*): spring, summer, fall, or winter.
> to flavor food (*v*): "I will *season* the stew with some oregano."
> to make experienced (*v*): "Several months in the touring company of a hit play will *season* a young actor because every night, he will learn something new about his craft."

WORD LIST 2

Now let's look at some new words and see how well you can recognize them—by noticing how they look and by determining what they do in the sentences in which they appear.

Here's what to do:

- Read all the sentences.
- Underline bold words you already know and can define by sight.
- Put a star over bold words that seem familiar but that you cannot define by sight.
- Circle words in bold that are unfamiliar to you.

Sentences

The attorney won **acquittal** because the prosecution couldn't make a strong enough case for a verdict of guilty.

He was accused of **negligence** because he ignored the safety of others by failing to remove the ice from his sidewalk.

The labor **contract** sought to guard union wages against **inflation**.

The **treaty** brought about needed **tranquility** in the area.

A college **periodical** published a paper evaluating performance and learning **parity** between campus-based and web-based chemistry courses.

parity

The **intruder** was handcuffed and led from the crime scene.

The businessman was accused of being a wartime **profiteer**.

profiteer

The **executor** of the estate told relatives of the deceased that they must accept the provisions of the will.

executor

Now look at the bold words in the sentences you just read. Fill in the information in the table that follows based only on what you know or can guess about each word. The first two words have been filled in for you to show you how it's done. You fill in the ones that have been left blank.

Word List 2: Practice Table

Word	Related Word	Part of Speech	Possible Meaning
acquittal	*acquit*	noun	found innocent of charges
negligence	*neglect*	noun	failure to act responsibly
contract			
inflation			
tranquility			
periodical			
parity			
intruder			
profiteer			
executor			

A CLOSER LOOK
Base Words and Related Words

Base words are complete words that are changed by the addition of beginnings or endings that may alter the final word's appearance or meaning. What are some other words suggested by the words in this lesson? In the blank column, write down words that are related to the indicated base words.

Lesson Words	Base Words	Related Words
1. acquittal	acquit	_____
2. negligence	neglect	_____
3. inflation	inflate	_____
4. tranquility	tranquil	_____
5. profiteer	profit	_____
6. periodical	period	_____

Words for the Wise

One of the interesting, but often frustrating, things about the English language is that many words have both *denotations* (literal meanings such as those you would find in a dictionary) and *connotations* (meanings that are associated with words as they are used for particular purposes). *Connotations* are like "flavors" that make meanings differ from one another. Some words have positive connotations; others have negative or neutral ones. For example, the words *fat*, *obese*, and *corpulent* may have cruel or unpleasant associations with (and for) people who are overweight, but the word *obese* may have a strictly clinical meaning to a medical professional. Words like *plump* and sometimes *fat* may evoke positive images of a big roasting turkey or a cheerful baby's cheeks. The denotations of all these words are practically identical, but the connotations are very different.

Look-Alikes

Circle the words in the groups that appear to be from the same family.

6. executor / execute / elocution / execrable

7. intrude / intrusion / intrusive / intrinsic

8. construction / contraction / contradiction / contractor

9. period / pureed / periodical / predicted

10. partial / party / parity / parent

Meanings for Word List 2

Now look at the words in this lesson. See how close the definitions you wrote in the practice table come to the ones that follow.

acquittal (uh-KWIT-uhl): the act of finding a defendant not guilty in a court of law

negligence (NEG-li-jens): habitual carelessness or failure to take proper action

contract (KON-trakt): a document that binds two or more people to an agreement; or (kun-TRAKT): to get smaller

inflation (in-FLAY-shun): the steady rise in prices that is directly related to an increased amount of money and credit in an economy

tranquility (tran-QUIL-ity): the state of being tranquil; serene

periodical (pe-ri-O-dik-uhl): a publication issued at regular intervals of more than one day

parity (PARE-i-tee): equality

intruder (in-TROO-duhr): someone who enters the property of another without permission

profiteer (prof-i-TEER): one who makes money on an unfortunate incident or situation

executor (ecks-EK-yoo-tore): one who represents the interests of a client's estate

PRACTICE EXERCISES

Now it's time to find out how well you know the words in this lesson.

Matching

Match the meanings in column B with the words in column A.

A	B
11. _____ executor	**a.** a regularly issued publication
12. _____ tranquility	**b.** an alliance or partnership
13. _____ negligence	**c.** failure to act responsibly
14. _____ periodical	**d.** state of serenity
15. _____ realists	**e.** people who judge by practical outcomes
16. _____ coalition	**f.** one who carries out the provisions of a will

Fill in the Blanks

Choose the correct word for each sentence.

17. The economy was troubled by _____, which decreased the buying power of most citizens.

18. The police believed that the same _____ had committed both crimes.

19. His own _____ in court gave him new faith in the justice system.

20. The union member refused to work without a _____.

21. His reputation as a wartime _____ made him unpopular.

22. Appointed as _____, she was bound by law to carry out the terms of the trust stipulated in her friend's will.

ANSWERS

Here are some of the ways you could apply the four approaches discussed in Lesson 1 to words from Word List 2.

Executor looks like the word *execute*. But be careful to distinguish the meaning of *executor* from *executioner*. These words derive from different meanings of the verb *execute*!

Profiteer sounds like the word *profit*.

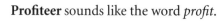

Periodical sounds like the word *period*.

The next page shows one way you could have filled in your table for Word List 2.

Word List 2: Answer Table

Word	Related Word	Part of Speech	Possible Meaning
acquittal	*acquit*	noun	found innocent of charges
negligence	*neglect*	noun	failure to act responsibly
contract	*contraction*, *contractor*	noun	an agreement between people (or getting smaller)
inflation	*inflate* like a balloon	noun (or verb)	process of getting larger
tranquility	*tranquil*	noun	a state of peace or serenity
periodical	*period*	noun	a publication issued at regular intervals
parity	*par* (an even number)	noun	being on the same foot as; equal
intruder	*intrude*	noun	someone who has entered a place illegally
profiteer	*profit*	noun	someone who makes money from someone else's difficulty
executor	*execute*	noun	someone who carries out someone else's wishes that were expressed in a will

A Closer Look

Base Words

1. acquitted
2. neglectful, negligent
3. inflatable, inflationary
4. tranquilize
5. profitable

Look-Alikes

6. executor, execute
7. intrude, intrusion, intrusive
8. contraction, contractor
9. period, periodical
10. partial, party

Practice Exercises

Matching

11. f
12. d
13. c
14. a
15. e
16. b

Fill in the Blanks

17. inflation
18. intruder
19. acquittal
20. contract
21. profiteer
22. executor

IN SHORT

In this lesson, you have had the opportunity to see how the visual image of a word can help you associate that word with a meaning. In the next lesson, you'll use these skills to determine the meaning of words from another area of interest: literature, the arts, and popular culture.

LESSON

3

WORDS FROM LITERATURE, THE ARTS, AND POPULAR CULTURE

In this lesson, you'll encounter another set of words, this time drawn from literature, the arts, and popular culture. You see and hear these words daily—in books, on television and the radio, and in the movies. You'll use your sight recognition skills to try to figure out their meaning.

How familiar do you think you are with words used in the art world or with the language of the entertainment industry? At the end of this lesson, you'll be comfortable with their vocabulary. When you find a word that you aren't sure of in this lesson, look closely at it and the role it plays in its sample sentence to discover the key to its meaning.

WORD LIST 3

What follows are sentences with this lesson's words in bold type. Again, here's what you do:

- Read all the sentences.
- Underline bold words you already know and can define by sight.
- Put a star over bold words that seem familiar but that you cannot define by sight.
- Circle words in bold that are unfamiliar to you.

Sentences

The Star Wars **trilogy** became a classic example of the science fiction adventure movie.

trilogy

Critics had great praise for the **retrospective** exhibition of the artist's work.

The artist's **studio** was filled with half-completed works and the smell of paint and turpentine.

studio

Most communities depend on contributions of wealthy **supporters** to sustain their cultural institutions.

Eduardo studied carefully the **vernacular** he would need to use in a **revival** of *Song of the South*.

The **miniseries** won the highest **ratings** of the year.

miniseries

Though the **celebrity** wrote his **memoirs** under a **pseudonym**, the **tabloid** newspapers revealed his identity.

The play contained a beautiful **soliloquy** by the leading actor.

Next, take a look at the words in bold from the sentences you just read, and in the table that follows, fill in the missing pieces by using your own personal knowledge of the words.

Word List 3: Practice Table

Word	In This Word, I See . . .	Part of Speech	Meaning
trilogy	*tri-* usually means "three"	noun	a three-part story
critic	*criticize*	noun	a person who judges program quality
retrospective			
studio			
supporter			
cultural			
vernacular			
revival			
miniseries			
ratings			
celebrity			
memoir			
pseudonym			
tabloid			
soliloquy			

A CLOSER LOOK
Word Forms

Most words have different forms, depending on their part of speech. You will learn more about how the part of speech affects a word in a later lesson, but for now, look at some of the words in this lesson as they appear in other forms.

Noun form	Verb form	Adjective form
critic	criticize	critical
He is a harsh *critic*.	Please don't *criticize* me.	He was in *critical* condition
supporter	support	supportive
He is a *supporter* of the arts.	Don't *support* that movement.	She was very *supportive* when her friends needed her.
culture	acculturate	cultural
He loved the *culture* of Japan.	She became *acculturated* to her new life.	She enjoyed the city's *cultural* life.

Words to the Wise

It is especially important to have a good sense of what words look like, because in English, so many words look different from the way they sound, and that makes it difficult to look up unfamiliar words in the dictionary. For example, if you had only heard the word *pseudonym*, you might reasonably think you should look in the dictionary under *su-* rather than *pseu-*. Similarly, if you had only heard the word *harassment*, you could quite understandably look in the dictionary under the *hu-* listings, rather than the *ha-* listings. One of the things that smart readers do is to get in the habit of really **looking at words** they see around them. Having a good mental image of words in general will help you recognize new words when you meet them.

The Right Form

To test yourself on word forms, circle the appropriate word to complete each of the following sentences. Be sure to use the form of the word required by its use in the sentence.

1. The retired general dictated his (memorize / memoirs) to his wife.

2. They all wanted the (celebrity / celebrate) to make an appearance on the stage.

3. Francis enjoyed the (cultured / cultural) activities of his new community.

4. He sought funding for a (revival / revive) of his favorite play.

5. Tamara read the reviews of the (criticisms / critics) in the daily papers.

Quick Recognition

Look quickly down this list of words. Choose the word in each pair that comes from Word List 3. Don't look back to check yourself until you have finished the whole group.

6. vernacular / vernacularly

7. solitary / soliloquy

8. introspective / retrospective

9. studio / studious

10. miniseries / miniature

11. rankings / ratings

12. tablet / tabloid

Meanings for Word List 3

This box gives the pronunciations and meanings for this lesson's words. How many did you know?

trilogy (TRIL-uh-jee): a story told in three parts

critic (KRIT-ik): a person who judges the artistic merit of theatrical or television performances and productions or any other artistic pursuits

retrospective (ret-roe-SPEK-tiv; n): an exhibition that reviews the entire career of an artist; or (RET-roe-spek-tiv; adj): looking back on the past

studio (STOO-dee-oh): a workspace in which an artist produces and shows his or her work

supporter (suh-PORT-er): one who supports or acts as a support. To support means to assist or help

cultural (KUL-chur-ul): pertaining to the artistic and intellectual life of a community

vernacular (ver-NAC-yoo-lehr): the everyday language spoken by people, or the variety of that language spoken by a specific group

revival (re-VIVE-ul): a presentation of a previously performed play

miniseries (MIN-ee-seer-eez): a story told in a short group of programs on television

ratings (RAY-tings): a system by which television programs, movies, and other products are judged for quality and consumer response

celebrity (suh-LEB-ri-tee): one who has achieved a high level of public recognition; or a high level of recognition

memoir (MEM-wahr): writings that reflect the writer's personal experiences in the past

pseudonym (SOO-duh-nim): a false name used to disguise identity

tabloid (TAB-loyd): newspapers that print sensational stories of doubtful authenticity, usually concerning celebrities

soliloquy (suh-LIL-oh-kwee): a speech given by a single speaker

PRACTICE EXERCISES

Test your memory of the words in this lesson.

True or False?

Mark following sentences as True or False, according to the meaning of the italicized words.

13. _____ A *tabloid* newspaper would emphasize financial news.

14. _____ A *trilogy* has three parts.

15. _____ A *retrospective* exhibition presents primarily an artist's newer work.

16. _____ A *supporter* of the theater is responsible for the management of the building.

17. _____ Moviegoers often depend on *critics* to help them choose which films to see.

Choose the Word

Circle the correct answer.

18. A system of judging works of art or entertainment:

(receipts / ratings / recalls)

19. A television story told in a few installments:

(pageant / miniseries / commercial)

20. A place where creative people work to produce their art:

(studio / campsite / laboratory)

21. A regional form of speech:

(dialogue / diatribe / vernacular)

22. The intellectual and artistic life of a community is its

(mercantile / urban / cultural) life.

ANSWERS

Here are ways you can use sight and a sense of structure to find clues to the meanings of some of the new words from this lesson.

Studio looks like *study*.

Miniseries has *mini-* in it, which usually means "short."

Trilogy contains *tri-*, which usually means "three."

Does your table look like the one shown on the next page?

Word List 3: Answer Table

Word	In This Word, I See . . .	Part of Speech	Meaning
trilogy	*tri-* usually means "three"	noun	a three-part story
critic	*criticize*	noun	a person who judges program quality
retrospective	*retro*	noun or adjective	a review of someone's past work; looking back
studio	*study*	noun	place where an artist works
supporter	*support*	noun	someone who supports something (helps, assists)
cultural	*culture*	noun	about the arts
vernacular	nothing familiar	noun	a special way of speaking

Word	In This Word, I See . . .	Part of Speech	Meaning
revival	*revive*	noun	something brought back to life, such as a play
miniseries	*mini-* usually means small	noun	a short series of programs
ratings	*rate*	noun	system showing how popular a show is
celebrity	*celebrate*	noun	someone who is easily recognized
memoir	*memory*	noun	personal memories
pseudonym	*name*	noun	a pen name
tabloid	nothing familiar	noun	newspaper that features gossip or scandal
soliloquy	*solitary*	noun	a speech by one person

A Closer Look

The Right Form

1. memoirs
2. celebrity
3. cultural
4. revival
5. critics

Quick Recognition

6. vernacular
7. soliloquy
8. retrospective
9. studio
10. miniseries
11. ratings
12. tabloid

Practice Exercises

True or False?

13. False
14. True
15. False
16. False
17. True

Choose the Word

18. ratings
19. miniseries
20. studio
21. vernacular
22. cultural

IN SHORT

With Lessons 2 and 3 completed, you should have a good idea of how to look for sight identification clues to word meanings. In the next lesson, you will start to listen to the sounds of words and discover how those sounds can help you figure out what unfamiliar words mean.

LESSON

4

WORD MEANING FROM SOUND

So far, you've used visual clues to decipher the meanings of new or unfamiliar words. In this lesson, you will
learn to use your ears to do the same thing to more
words in the fields of art, literature, and popular culture. And you'll learn some of the rules of phonics to
assist you in sounding out words.

How you recognize words depends a lot on
how well you can "hear" each sound in them when you meet them in
print. Even when you recognize a word by sight, you usually do so because you have
a sense of the sounds that are represented by the letter combinations that you see.
The relationship between letters and sounds is called *phonics.*

VOWELS

Remember, the vowels are *a, e, i, o, u,* and sometimes *y.*

Long Vowels

Vowels that are long say their own names; in other words, a vowel that is long sounds just like the letter as you would say it in the alphabet. Note the long vowel sounds in boldface in the following words:

r**a**tings	profit**ee**r	rev**i**val	p**u**rity

Short Vowels

On the other hand, short vowels have other sounds. They sound like the first sounds in *ant, enter, inch, ostrich,* and *under.* Look at the bolded short vowels in the following:

expedite	tr**i**logy	c**o**ntr**a**ct

The Schwa Sound

The schwa sound, which is noted in the dictionary as an upside-down *e,* signals a neutral vowel sound that we hear as "uh." (The word *schwa* is pronounced SHWAH.) In the following words, the schwa sounds are bolded. Note that they occur in unaccented syllables:

st**a**bility	reviv**a**l	cel**e**brity	tril**o**gy

Vowel Combinations

In grade school, you probably learned the saying, "When two vowels go walking, the first one does the talking and says its own name." Notice how this rule applies in words like *plaintiff,* for example, where the two vowels *ai* combine to make the long *a* sound. Here are some other words that have double-vowel combinations that carry the long sound of the first vowel:

gru**e**some	fl**o**at	l**i**e	tr**ue**
eager	gr**ai**n	pl**ea**se	fr**ai**l

There are exceptions to this rule, however. (There are *always* exceptions in English, as we know too well!) When the letter *i* is the first letter, it often stands alone and each vowel makes its own sound. Thus, we hear "hye-AY-tuss," not simply "hye-tuss," in the word h*ia*tus.

The *y* Sounds

The letter *y* has several sounds in words:

- It can sound like short *i*, as in pseudonym (SOO-doe-nim)
- It can sound like long *e*, as in trilogy (TRI-luh-gee).
- It can sound like long *i*, as in cycle (SEYE-kul)
- We also hear the letter *y* with the yuh sound that begins such words as *youth*.

CONSONANTS AND CONSONANT COMBINATIONS

Consonants also break the sound rules, with their exceptions.

Hard and Soft *c* and *g*

The letters *c* and *g* can be soft or hard. When the *c* is soft, it sounds like *s*. When it has the hard sound, it's like *k*. When *g* is soft, it carries the *j* sound. And when it is hard, it sounds like the first sound in *green* or *gasoline.*

Fortunately, there is a handy rule that helps you to deal with these sounds when you meet them in unfamiliar words: In general, *c* and *g* sounds are usually soft (the *s* and *j* sounds) when they are followed by the letters *e*, *i*, or *y*. Otherwise, they are hard.

- In words like *city* or *celebrity,* we hear the *c* with the *s* sound.
- In the word *critic,* the first *c* carries the *k* sound (by the way, so does the last *c*).
- Some *g* words that follow the rule are *generous* and *gentle,* with their soft *j* sounds.
- Words like *goodness* and *game,* as you would predict, begin with the hard *g* sound.

There are a few exceptions to the *e* and *i* rule with the letter *g*. These words have hard *g* sounds: *get, girl.*

Silent Consonants

Often, in English, you see consonants that you don't hear when the words are said. Obvious examples are the silent *gh* combinations found in words like *flight* and *through*. Other times, one consonant in a combination is silent and the other does the talking: Thus, the *p* in **pseudonym** and the *h* in **ghost** are seen but not heard.

Consonant Combinations

Consonants that work together to make a single sound include *sh*, *th*, and *ch*. These are called *digraphs*. Sometimes, they have different sounds, depending on the word:

> The *sh* sound in **push**
>
> The *th* sound in **that**, which is different from the *th* sound in **thought**
>
> The *ch* sound in **chair**

Words for the Wise

A word about phonetic spellings: The words presented in this book use a simplified phonetic spelling that tells how each word sounds. Note that the part of the phonetic spelling in CAPITAL letters carries the accent, or stress, in the pronunciation of the word. In the dictionary, you will often find a more technical kind of pronunciation key for the phonetic spellings of words you are seeking. Since many dictionaries have slightly different presentations of phonetic symbols, the best thing you can do when you look in a dictionary is to look at its symbol code, which is usually printed near the front of the book. The phonetic key for this book appears on page ix.

DIVIDING PHONETICS INTO SYLLABLES

Now that you have had a quick review of some of the basic sound combinations that words contain, it's time to use that knowledge to decode, or sound out, unfamiliar words.

Syllables (pronounced *SILL-uh-bulls*) are the parts of words that carry separate sounds. They may be made up of one, or more than one, letter, but *every syllable must have a vowel sound*. Breaking words down into individual syllables is one of the best ways for picking out the individual sounds in the word. It also helps you to divide and conquer long words that look scary at first sight.

Here are some strategies for breaking words into syllables.

- Divide words between two consonants:

    fas-ter   at-ti-tude

    en-ding

- Divide words after prefixes (word beginnings) and before suffixes (word endings):

    pre-mo-ni-*tion*   *un*-mind-*ful*

    sub-trac-*tion*

- If a word ends in *le*, the consonant just before the *l* is the first letter of the last syllable:

    trem-*ble*   be-lit-*tle*

If you already have a good sense of how a word sounds, you can divide it on the basis of the sound of its vowels.

- Divide after the vowel if the syllable has a long sound. This kind of sylla-ble is called an *open syllable*:

    st*u*-di-o   h*u*-mid

    r*a*-tings   mis-t*a*-ken-ly

    c*e*-dar

- Divide after the consonant if the syllable has a short sound. This kind of syllable is called a *closed syllable*:

    v*e*r-n*a*c-u-lar   wh*i*s-per

    cr*i*t-*i*c   f*a*n-t*a*s-tic

WORD LIST 4

Now look at some more words drawn from the arts, literature, and popular cul-ture and apply what you know about phonetic approaches to these words. You know what to do:

- Read all the sentences.
- Underline bold words you already know and can define by sight.

- Put a star over bold words that seem familiar but that you cannot define by sight.
- Circle words in bold that are unfamiliar to you.

tycoon

Sentences

The famous movie **tycoon** declared he had a "three-picture deal" with a major action star.

Pearl had a brief **cameo** role in the made-for-television movie.

Audrey watched **cinema** greats from the Golden Age of Hollywood gather for the awards ceremony.

Saturday Night Live has a number of **opponents** that are challenging its place as the primary site for political satire on television.

The author's **anthology** contained a superb collection of new short stories.

improvisation

The comedian received great **commendation** for his performance, which involved **improvisations** based on audience requests.

The television series taped three new **episodes** before it went on **hiatus** for two months.

Now take a closer look at the words in bold from the preceding sentences. Fill in the needed information in the Word List 4: Practice Table. Notice that you do not see phonetic spellings in the table. First try to apply your own knowledge of phonics to figure out how the words sound. Use the sentences to help you figure out what each bold word means. The first two are done for you.

Word List 4: Practice Table

Word	Syllables	Vowel Sounds	Meaning
tycoon	ty-coon	long *i*, long *oo*	powerful executive
cameo	cam-e-o	short *a*, longe *e*, long *o*	a brief role in a movie
cinema			
opponent			
satire			
anthology			
commendation			
improvisation			
episode			
hiatus			

A CLOSER LOOK
Consonants

1. In the word *cinema*, the *c* probably has the sound of the letter _____ because

_____.

2. In the word *tycoon*, the *c* has the hard/soft (circle one) sound because

_____.

3. The *th* in the word *anthology* has the same sound as the *th* in the word

_____.

4. The *c* in *civil* has the sound of letter _____.

Word Forms

5. The verb form of the word *satire* is _____.
6. The verb form of the word *improvisation* is _____.

Who Am I?

7. I am a homograph, or a word that has two distinct meanings or derivations. I can mean a jewelry style featuring one image carved on top of another, or I can mean a brief, often uncredited, role in a movie. I am a(n) _____.

8. I am a Greek word that means gap or opening. Television viewers miss their shows while I am around. I am a(n) _____.

9. I am a competitor for prizes or awards. A synonym for me is enemy or challenger. I am a(n) _____.

10. I am one part of a television series. I show one part of a story or a new installment of a story. I am a(n) _____.

Meanings for Word List 4

Here are this lesson's words with their pronunciations and meanings. How many did you get right?

tycoon (tye-COON): a person who has a lot of money and power

cameo (KAM-ee-oh): a brief, often uncredited role in a movie or television program. It can also mean a style of jewelry in which a stone appears with one image carved on top of another

cinema (SIN-e-muh): a movie or motion picture

opponent (uh-POE-nuhnt): one that opposes another or others in a debate, battle, sport, or other competition

satire (SAT-eyer): a kind of writing that makes fun of institutions, people, or events as a form of criticism

anthology (an-THOL-uh-jee): a collection of writings

commendation (CAHM-en-dae-shun): something that commends; an award or other citation

improvisation (im-prov-iz-AY-shun): an unrehearsed performance

episode (EP-i-sode): one segment in a series on television, or a specific event in history

hiatus (hye-AY-tuss): a period of time between activities; an interval

PRACTICE EXERCISES

Test your memory of the words in this lesson.

Best Definition

Circle the best definition for each of the following words.

11. episode   letter / part of a whole / book

12. anthology   earth science / collection / study of mankind

13. hiatus   vegetable / lung disease / interval

14. improvisation   unrehearsed performance / poor performance / better performance

15. cinema   spice / motion picture / sports car

Opposites

Circle the word that means the opposite of the first word in each line.

16. commendation   praise / musical instruments / criticism

17. opponents   competitors / companions / coworkers

18. tycoon   pauper / power broker / star

19. satire   comedy / circus act / drama

20. cameo   lead / promotion / anchorman

Unscramble

Unscramble the letters to find the words from Word List 4.

21. nopnepot   _____

22. suthia   _____

23. yctono   _____

24. resitra   _____

25. manice   _____

ANSWERS

Here are two clues to the meanings of words in this lesson:

Improvisation looks like *improvise.*

Because **tycoon** is an unfamiliar word, you would most likely need to know the context in which it appears to help understand its meaning. *Tycoon* originated from Japanese, which in turn had borrowed it from Chinese where it meant "great prince." The Japanese used the word to make the shogun—the commander in chief of the Japanese army—more imposing to foreign visitors.

Does your filled-in table look like the one shown here?

Word List 4: Answer Table

Word	Syllables	Vowel Sounds	Meaning
tycoon	ty-coon	long *i*, long *oo*	powerful executive
cameo	cam-e-o	short *a*, longe *e*, long *o*	a brief role in a movie
cinema	cin-e-ma	short *i*, schwa *e*, schwa *a*	a movie
opponent	op-po-nent	schwa *u*, long *o*, schwa *e*	competitor
satire	sat-ire	short *a*, long *i*,	a show that makes fun of people and situations
anthology	an-thol-o-gy	short *a*, short *o*, schwa *o*	a collection of stories
commendation	com-men-da-tion	short *o*, schwa *e*, schwa *o*	praises
improvisation	im-prov-i-sa-tion	short *i*, short *o*, short *i*, long *a*	unplanned performance

episode	ep-i-sode	short *e*, short *i*, long *o*	part of a series
hiatus	hi-a-tus	long *i*, long *a*, short *u*	an interval or gap in time

A Closer Look

Consonants

1. *s* sound

The *c* is followed by *i*.

2. hard sound

The *c* is not followed by *e*, *i*, or *y*.

3. *th* sound in *thought*

4. *s* sound

Word Forms

5. satirize

6. improvise

Who Am I?

7. cameo

8. hiatus

9. opponent

10. episode

Practice Exercises

Best Definition

11. part of a whole

12. collection

13. interval

14. unrehearsed performance

15. motion picture

Unscramble

21. opponent

22. hiatus

23. tycoon

24. satire

25. cinema

Opposites

16. criticism

17. coworkers

18. pauper

19. drama

20. lead

IN SHORT

In this lesson, you discovered that familiar words can give clues to the meanings of unfamiliar words simply because they sound alike. In Lesson 5, you will begin to use another kind of clue—the *structure* of a word—to get to its meaning.

WORDS FROM SCIENCE AND TECHNOLOGY

In this lesson, you will encounter words drawn from science and technology. They're typical of the kind of vocabulary you'd find in newspaper and magazine accounts of current advances in these fields.

Use again your strategies of sight, sound, and context to unlock the meanings of the new words here. Later in the lesson, you will begin to see how words are structured and how parts of words, like word roots, can give you other clues to meaning. This will prepare you for the rest of the structural clues coming up in the following lessons.

WORD LIST 5

As you read the words in the sentences on the next page, think about how you would approach unfamiliar scientific and technical words. Look for sight and sound clues that could clarify their meaning for you. As before, here's what you do:

- Read all the sentences.
- Underline bold words you already know and can define by sight.

- Put a star over bold words that seem familiar but that you cannot define by sight.
- Circle words in bold that are unfamiliar to you.

Sentences

Environmentalists have defended their **theory** about **global warming**, the proposition that holes in the ozone layer will create significant changes in weather patterns.

Following the failure of **in vitro** fertilization to result in a pregnancy, the couple decided to seek a **surrogate** mother to bear them a child.

Practitioners of **holistic** medicine believe that the whole person should be considered in the treatment plan.

cloning

Many were concerned that clear-cutting forest land would threaten the wildlife **ecosystem**, driving animals from their natural living spaces.

The subject of **cloning**—that is, asexual reproduction that brings about an identical genetic duplicate of the original organism—is highly controversial.

The researcher found that the substance was an effective **catalyst** that brought about a significant change in the chemical composition of the drug.

Recently, new **digital** technology, in which electronic images are converted into electronic bits by computer, has permitted amazing special effects in the movies.

The hybridizing of the two rose types created a **crossbreed** that invited much interest among botanists and nurserymen.

Though the tobacco industry has insisted that the nicotine in cigarettes contains no **carcinogens**, it is nevertheless widely assumed that components of nicotine do cause cancer.

The scientist had studied jellyfish and starfish for many years. His fascination with **invertebrates** never diminished.

invertebrates

That was the most **virulent** strain of influenza ever seen by U.S. health officials. The strength and seriousness of the illness was devastating.

virulent

Ben and Hernando observed the **kinetic** energy of the object as it rolled down the incline. Energy of motion was the key topic that day in class.

One of the most exciting studies in science today is the **genome** project, in which human genes are mapped to study their individual structures.

Now look again at the bold words in the sentences you just read and fill in the information about them in the table on the next page. Try your hand at phonetic spelling for column 2 by using what you know about how words sound. Refer to the phonetic spelling guide on page ix.

A CLOSER LOOK
Completions

Fill in the correct word from Word List 5.

1. Scientists who study the earth's temperature are divided in their opinions regarding the problem of _____.

2. Plants that have been hybridized are known as _____ .

3. Animals that do not have a backbone or spine are called

_____.

4. Doctors rely on _____ fertilization as one treatment for couples who are having difficulty conceiving a child.

5. An experiment that studies the movement of atomic particles is a

_____ study.

Phonics

Fill in the blanks to describe how the letters sound.

6. The letter *c* in the word *catalyst* probably sounds like the letter ____ because

_____.

7. The letter *g* in *genome* probably sounds like the letter _____ because

_____.

8. The letter *a* in the word *digital* is (long / short / schwa).

9. The second letter *c* in the word *carcinogen* sounds like the letter ____ because

_____.

10. All of the vowels in the word *kinetic* are (long / short / schwa).

A Preview of Word Structure

Many of the words in this lesson can best be approached by sight, sound, or context. Before leaving this list, however, look more closely at how some of the words are made up and how their structure can help you to connect them with other words.

Word List 5: Practice Table

Word	Pronunciation	Part of Speech
theory	THEE-uh-ree	noun
global warming	gloh-bul WAHR-ming	noun
in vitro	in VEET-roh	adjective
surrogate		
holistic		
ecosystem		
cloning		
catalyst		
digital		
crossbreed		
carcinogen		
invertebrates		
virulent		
kinetic		
genome		

For example, look at the word *genome*. The *gen-* in *genome* refers to the Latin word *genus*, which means "type" or "category." That same part or root of the word appears in many other words that have something to do with groups or families of people:

***gen*ealogy**	the study of family lineage
***gen*ocide**	the destruction of a particular people
***gen*etics**	the study of family characteristics
primo***gen*iture**	the state of being first in the line of a family
***gen*eration**	one period in a family's history

You will see this root later in the French word ***gen*re** in Lesson 14.

Now consider the word *kinetic*. The source of this word is the Greek root *kino*, which means movement or motion. Here are some other words that share that part of the word and the meaning carried by that word part:

***kine*siology**	the study of the motion of the human body
***kine*scope**	an early form of television in which a moving image was made on a picture tube
hyper***kine*sis**	a condition in which a person, usually a child, is excessively active or energetic

In Lesson 4, you've seen the French form of this word in ***cine*ma**, a moving picture. Lesson 6 will focus on other such word roots that help signal meaning to the reader.

Meanings for Word List 5

Here are the words and definitions for this lesson. See how well you figured out the meanings and sound of words through phonetic spellings.

theory (THEE-uh-ree): a set of statements or principles used to explain a phenomena, usually one that has been tested repeatedly or is widely accepted

global warming (GLOH-bul WAHR-ming): the possibility that the earth's surface and weather patterns will be affected by changes in the earth's atmosphere

in vitro (in VEET-roh): outside of the body. In Latin, this phrase means "in glass," and the term itself is sometimes (incorrectly) defined as the means to a "test tube baby"

surrogate (SUR-oh-guht): a substitute or replacement, or one who is a legal sponsor for a child. In legal usage, a surrogate court is one that deals with custody and/or adoption cases

holistic (hoh-LIS-tik): the medical practice that concerns itself with the whole person—physically, psychologically, and emotionally

ecosystem (EE-koe-sis-tuhm): a grouping of living things and the environment in which they live and interact

cloning (KLOHN-ing): asexual reproduction of an exact genetic duplicate of an organism. This term is also used to describe the process of duplicating the components of computers

catalyst (KAT-uh-list): in science, a substance that brings about a chemical change. In human relations, a catalyst can be a person or event that effects a change of behavior

digital (DIJ-i-tuhl): pertaining to a kind of technology in which symbols are converted to electronic bits that can then be read by a computer.

crossbreed (KRAHS-breed): an organism produced by the mating of two different species, breeds, or varieties

carcinogen (kahr-SIN-uh-jen): a cancer-causing substance

invertebrates (in-VUHR-tuh-brayts): animals that do not possess a spinal column

virulent (VEER-yoo-luhnt): having a devastating and fast-spreading effect; malignant

kinetic (kin-ET-ik): related to motion or movement

genome (JEE-nohm): the individual structure of human genes that carry the characteristics of the organism

PRACTICE EXERCISES

Try out your mastery of the words in this lesson.

Fill in the Blanks

In the following words, fill in the missing letters.

11. The baby was born after her parents had undergone in __ __tro fertilization.

12. A forest is an eco _ _ _ tem that contains plants and animals interacting with one another.

13. Albert Einstein introduced the the __ _ y of relativity.

14. The judge in the surr __ __ ate court ruled on the adoption.

15. The most colorful flowers in the show were the new cr__ __ sbreeds from France.

True or False?

Mark the following statements True or False, according to the meanings of the italicized words.

16. _____ *Global warming* means that the Ice Age is over.

17. _____ A *catalyst* is a financial advisor.

18. _____ *Digital* technology is out of fashion.

19. _____ Medical *cloning* is a highly controversial subject in science today.

20. _____ *Holistic* practitioners are concerned with all aspects of a person's life.

ANSWERS

Here are three examples of how to approach some words in this lesson to determine their meaning.

Virulent looks like *virus*.

Invertebrates sounds like *vertebra*.

Cloning would need a context to clarify.

Word List 5: Answer Table

Word	Pronunciation	Part of Speech
theory	THEE-uh-ree	noun
global warming	gloh-bul WAHR-ming	noun
in vitro	in VEET-roh	adjective
surrogate	SUR-oh-guht	adjective
holistic	hoh-LIS-tik	adjective
ecosystem	EE-koe-sis-tuhm	noun
cloning	KLOHN-ing	noun
catalyst	KAT-uh-list	noun
digital	DIJ-i-tul	adjective
crossbreed	KRAHS-breed	noun
carcinogen	kahr-SIN-uh-jen	noun
inverterbrates	in-VUHR-tuh-brayts	noun
virulent	VEER-yoo-luhnt	adjective
kinetic	kin-ET-ik	adjective
genome	JEE-nohm	adjective

A Closer Look

Completions

1. global warming

2. crossbreeds

3. invertebrates

4. in vitro

5. kinetic

Phonics

6. *k*, the *c* is not followed by *e*, *i*, or *y*.

7. *j*, the *g* is followed by an *e*.

8. schwa

9. *s*, the *c* is followed by an *i*.

10. short

Practice Exercises

Fill in the Blanks

11. in *vi*tro

12. eco*sy*stem

13. the*ory*

14. surro*g*ate

15. cr*oss*breeds

True or False?

16. False

17. False

18. False

19. True

20. True

IN SHORT

In this lesson, you met words from the fields of science and technology and began to look at the structure of words to determine their meaning. In the next lesson, you will meet the first of a number of root words on which many other words are built.

LESSON

WORD MEANING FROM STRUCTURE

In Lesson 1, you looked at the broad view of approaches to figuring out unfamiliar words. You noticed several "structural clues"—prefixes, suffixes, and roots—in words that could help you recognize their meaning. In this lesson, you will take a closer look at word roots. In later lessons, you will look at the other parts of words that change or add to meaning.

Roots are the pieces of words that carry direct meaning. Generally, the roots that are the basis of words in English are from the Greek or the Latin. Because so many words in English grow from these root systems, knowing some of the most commonly used roots gives you access to many words at once. When you combine your knowledge of roots in this lesson and the next with your knowledge of suffixes and prefixes in the lessons that follow, you'll have the key to the meanings of literally hundreds of words.

Notice that roots are different base words, which you encountered in Lesson 2. Base words are whole words that have various forms. Roots are only **parts** of words that alert the reader to the meaning of the whole word. They are sometimes called "combining forms." You have already met several words that contain interesting roots or elements; they include *femin*ist, *frater*nization, *sur*ro*gate*, and *con*tract.

WORD LIST 6

What follows are a number of words in bold, also from the fields of science and technology, that contain word roots. The roots of these bold words are indicated. Later in the lesson, you will see how those roots appear in other words as well.

You know what to do:

- Read all the sentences.
- Underline bold words you already know and can define by sight.
- Put a star over bold words that seem familiar but that you cannot define by sight.
- Circle words in bold that are unfamiliar to you.

Sentences

The two species had a **sym*biotic*** relationship in that they lived in a close relationship to which both contributed equally.

The rapid ***mu*tation** of the viruses made treatment difficult. Such changes in the characteristics of the cells made the doctors very anxious.

metric

Though common in Europe, the ***metric*** system, a decimal system of weights and measures, has never been successfully adopted by American society.

Washing your hands frequently can help keep you from getting sick, as soap and water can destroy many types of ***path*ogens**.

hydraulic

The ***hydr*aulic** brakes made a terrible sound as the truck slid down the hill.

A ***philo*sopher** seeks reason and truth through thinking, reading, and writing.

In October 1947, while working on Rusinga Island, ***archae*ologist** Mary Leakey unearthed the fossil skull of the primate Proconsul africanus, the first ape ever to be found.

dormant

Some viruses lie ***dorm*ant**, or inactive, for many years.

The winter ***sol*stice** takes place on December 21 or 22. In North America, it marks the shortest day of the year, when the sun is at the farthest point south of the equator.

The table on the next page shows you how the roots that appear in words show up in other words as well. Fill in the phonetic spellings and the parts of speech on the basis of your knowledge of the sight and sound clues you've learned so far.

Words to the Wise

Word roots can be a little confusing. Sometimes, two roots look the same but have different meanings. For example, in addition to the root *sol* that means "sun," there is another word root *sol* that instead means "alone," not "sun." From this other root, we get:

> *solitary*—by one's self
>
> *solitude*—time spent alone
>
> *solo*—a song sung alone
>
> *soliloquy*—speech spoken alone (as you'll remember from
>   Lesson 3)

A CLOSER LOOK

More Rooting Around

Look again at some of the roots in the words in this lesson. What other words do you know that might be based on these word parts?

Draw a line between the words in column A and their meanings in column B.

A	B
1. _____*phil*osophy	**a.** power provided by water
2. _____*path*os	**b.** extreme feelings
3. _____*arch*aic	**c.** goodwill to fellow humans
4. _____*prim*ogeniture	**d.** the study of logics and ethics
5. _____*phil*anthropy	**e.** antiquated
6. _____*hydro*electric	**f.** the rights of the first born

Word List 6: Practice Table

Word	Root Meaning	Words That Share the Root	Phonetic Spelling	Part of Speech
sym*bio*tic	life	*biology*, the study of living things; *antibiotics*, drugs that destroy harmful bacteria	sim-bee-OT-ik	adjective
*mut*ation	change	*mutant*, a plant or animal whose inherited characteristics have undergone a change	myoo-tay-shun	noun
*met*ric	measure	*diameter*, the measure across a circle that divides it into two halves; *thermometer*, a device that measures temperature		
*path*ogen	suffering	*pathology*, the study of disease; *pathos*, an emotion of sympathetic pity		
*hydr*aulic	water	hydrant, a large water faucet; hydrophobia, fear of water		
*phil*osopher	love	*philharmonic*, symphony orchestra; *philology*, love of learning and literature		
*archa*eologist	ancient	*archaeoastronomy*, the study of the astronomy of ancient cultures; *archaebacterium*, any of a class of primitive bacteria		
*pri*mate	first	*primer*, a first book; *primitive*, a first form		
*dorm*ant	sleep	*dormitory*, a place where students sleep; *dormer*, a bedroom window		
*sol*stice	sun	*solar*, pertains to the sun; *solarium*, a sun room		

Syllables

In the table, you broke words down phonetically. Here, divide some of them into syllables using the rules from Lesson 4.

7. symbiotic _____

8. solstice _____

9. metric _____

10. mutation _____

11. dormant _____

Meanings for Word List 6

This box shows the words from this lesson with their pronunciations and meanings. How many do you know?

symbiotic (sym-bee-OT-ik): mutually dependent

mutation (myoo-TAY-shun): a change in the form or nature of something

metric (MET-rik): a decimal system of weights and measures

pathogen (PA-thuh-jen): a disease causing agent, such as a bacterium or virus

hydraulic (hye-DRAW-lik): operated by the force of water or some other liquid

philosopher (fuh-LAW-suh-fer): a person who seeks wisdom or enlightenment

archaeologist (ahr-kaye-AW-luh-jist): one who studies material remains of past human life and activities

primate (PRY-mayt): the highest form of mammal

dormant (DOR-muhnt): at rest or inactive

solstice (SOL-stis): the days on which the sun is farthest from the equator (December 22 and June 21)

PRACTICE EXERCISES

Test your memory of the words in this lesson.

True or False?

Mark the following sentences as True or False according to the meanings of the italicized words.

12. _____ An example of a *pathogen* would be a flu virus.

13. _____ *Mutations* could create virulent diseases.

14. _____ An *archaeologist* would study the solar system.

15. _____ The sun shines all day on the winter *solstice* throughout North America.

16. _____ A *symbiotic* relationship is one in which each person in the relationship is very independent.

Fill in the Blanks

Choose the correct word to complete these sentences.

17. A _____ would seek to become wiser through reasoning.

18. A(n) _____ volcano would be inactive.

19. Kilograms and liters are part of the _____ system of measurement.

20. A human is a(n) _____ because humans are of the first, or highest, species.

21. A(n) _____ brake system uses the power of water.

ANSWERS

Here's how some clues can be used to determine the meaning of some of the words in this lesson:

 Dormant looks like *dormitory*.

 Metric looks like *meter*.

 Hydraulic has the same beginning as *hydrant*.

Check your table with the version on the next page.

Word List 6: Answer Table

Word	Root Meaning	Words That Share the Root	Phonetic Spelling	Part of Speech
sym**bio**tic	life	*biology*, the study of living things; *antibiotics*, drugs that destroy harmful bacteria	sim-bee-OT-ik	adjective
***mut**ation*	change	*mutant*, a plant or animal whose inherited characteristics have undergone a change	myoo-tay-shun	noun
***met**ric*	measure	*diameter*, the measure across a circle that divides it into two halves; *thermometer*, a device that measures temperature	MET-rik	adjective
***path**ogen*	suffering	*pathology*, the study of disease; *pathos*, an emotion of sympathetic pity	PA-thu-jen	noun
***hydr**aulic*	water	hydrant, a large water faucet; hydrophobia, fear of water	hye-DRAW-lik	adjective
***phil**osopher*	love	*philharmonic*, symphony orchestra; *philology*, love of learning and literature	fuh-LAW-suh-fer	noun
***archa**eologist*	ancient	*archaeoastronomy*, the study of the astronomy of ancient cultures; *archaebacterium*, any of a class of primitive bacteria	ahr-kaye-AW-luh-jist	noun
***pri**mate*	first	*primer*, a first book; *primitive*, a first form	PRYE-mayt	noun
***dorm**ant*	sleep	*dormitory*, a place where students sleep; *dormer*, a bedroom window	DOR-muhnt	adjective
***sol**stice*	sun	*solar*, pertains to the sun; *solarium*, a sun room	SOL-stis	noun

A Closer Look

More Rooting Around

1. d
2. b
3. e
4. f
5. c
6. a

Syllables

7. sym-bi-ot-ic
8. sol-stice
9. met-ric
10. mu-ta-tion
11. dor-mant

Practice Exercises

True or False?

12. True
13. True
14. False
15. False
16. False

Fill in the Blank

17. philosopher
18. dormant
19. metric
20. primate
21. hydraulic

IN SHORT

In this lesson, you have seen how recognizing roots of words helps determine their meaning. In the next lesson, you will meet some more word roots that will give you clues to the meaning of many words that appear in print almost daily in articles, brochures, and books related to healthcare.

7

WORDS FROM MEDICINE AND HEALTHCARE

The words in this lesson have to do with medicine and healthcare. Look for clues to their meaning by sight, sound, and structure. And be on the lookout for word roots you may know from other words.

The number of technical and medical words in the language grows every year as new words are added to describe previously unknown advances or techniques. The challenge of learning such words can be made fun by applying the vocabulary-building skills you have already learned. You've probably heard many of the words in this lesson—words associated with the healthcare field—but you may not be sure of their exact meaning. As you read them, try to make connections to other words or word roots that you already know. Familiar words can lead you to the meaning of those in this lesson's list.

WORD LIST 7

The following are sentences with words from this lesson's word list in bold. You know what to do:

- Read all the sentences.
- Underline bold words you already know and can define by sight.
- Put a star over bold words that seem familiar but that you cannot define by sight.
- Circle words in bold that are unfamiliar to you.

Sentences

The fetus could not be considered viable after only 20 weeks **gestation**.

The injured man was fitted with a **prosthesis** that looked almost identical to the arm he had lost in the accident.

The **coroner** who examined the body said that the cause of death was a gunshot wound to the chest.

Though he had contracted tuberculosis as a child, it took many years before the symptoms of the disease **manifested** themselves.

It takes most people a long time to **convalesce** after a stroke.

Their benefits plan at work allowed for a **recompense** of medical expenses.

immune

He thought he was **immune** to measles because, although he had been exposed to the disease many times, he had never broken out in spots.

The woman, **debilitated** from her long ordeal, was eligible for **Medicare** because she was over age 65.

The doctors feared a **pandemic**, so they ordered those who had contracted the virus to be **quarantined**.

therapeutic

The return of the father after so long an absence had a **therapeutic** effect on all the relationships in the family. Everyone was happier and more relaxed.

The nurses in the **triage** unit separated the **trauma** cases—those most seriously injured in the multicar accident—for the fastest attention by the medical staff.

triage

Despite the efforts of the pathologists to trace the **etiology** of the disease, its origins remained a mystery.

Now take a closer look at the words in bold. Fill in the needed information on the table on the next page.

A CLOSER LOOK
Sound Clues
Fill in the blanks in the sentences, using your knowledge of phonetics.

1. In the word *gestation*, the letter *g* carries the _____ sound because

_____.

2. The letter *c* in *coroner* carries the _____ sound because

_____.

3. In the word *pandemic*, the letter *c* has the _____ sound because

_____.

4. In the word *convalesce*, the second *c* has the _____ sound because

_____.

5. In the word *triage*, the letter *g* has the _____ sound because

_____.

Sight and Structure Clues
What do you see in the words?

6. *Therapeutic* probably is a form of the word _____.

7. We see the word *immune* in another word:_____.

8. *Medicare* is a word blended from two other words: _____ and

_____.

9. The prefix *re-* in *recompense* usually means "back" or "again." To recompense is to _____.

10. The suffix *-ology*, as in the word *etiology* or *biology*, usually means

_____.

Word List 7: Practice Table

Word	Pronunciation	Part of Speech	Possible Meaning
gestation	jes-TAY-shun	noun	time in the uterus
prosthesis	pros-THEE-sis	noun	artificial body part
coroner	KOR-uhn-er	noun	medical examiner
manifest	MA-nuh-fest		
convalesce	kon-vuh-LESS		
recompense	re-KUHM-pents		
immune	im-MYOON		
debillitated	duh-BIL-i-tay-ted		
Medicare	MED-i-kare		
pandemic	pan-DEM-ik		
quarantined	KWAHR-un-teend		
therapeutic	ther-ah-PYOO-tik		
etiology	ee-tee-OL-uh-jee		
triage	TREE-ahj		
trauma	TRAH-muh		

Meanings for Word List 7

See how well you were able to unlock the meaning of the words. Here they are with their pronunciations and meanings.

gestation (jes-TAY-shun): the length of a pregnancy or time spent in the uterus

prosthesis (pros-THEE-sis): a replacement or artificial form of a body part

coroner (KOR-uhn-er): a physician who examines a body after death

manifest (MA-nuh-fest): to make evident by showing or displaying

convalesce (kon-vuh-LESS): to return to health after illness

recompense (re-KUHM-pents): payment in return for something

immune (im-MYOON): protected against something harmful

debilitated (duh-BILL-i-tay-ted): weakened

Medicare (MED-i-kare): a federal subsidy for the cost of medical care of elderly people

pandemic (pan-DEM-ic): widespread; epidemic over a large geographic region

quarantined (KWAHR-un-teend): isolated from others to prevent the spread of illness

therapeutic (ther-ah-PYOO-tik): having a favorable change in physical or mental health

etiology (ee-tee-OL-uh-jee): the study of the origin or cause of illnesses

triage (TREE-ahj): the process by which the most severely injured are singled out for prompt treatment (originally performed by separating the injured according to three orders of priority)

trauma (TROW-muh): severe shock or anxiety

PRACTICE EXERCISES

Now it's time to test yourself on the words.

Scrambled Letters

Here are five words from Word List 7 that have their letters scrambled. Can you determine what they are?

11. egitra _____

12. ronecor _____

13. matuar _____

14. mcinpead _____

15. euimmn _____

True or False?

Mark the following sentences as True or False on the basis of the meanings of the italicized words.

16. _____ A *quarantine* might be in effect during a *pandemic*.

17. _____ If we know the *etiology* of an illness, we know its *symptoms*.

18. _____ A *debilitated* person has a new lease on life.

19. _____ A *prosthesis* is the summary of an article in a medical journal.

20. _____ A *therapeutic* environment helps someone recover from an illness.

ANSWERS

Here are the ways you could use the four approaches you have learned to decode some of the words in Word List 7.

Therapeutic looks like *therapy*.

Triage begins with *tri-*, which usually means "three."

Immune looks like *immunization*.

Does your filled-in table for this lesson look similar to the one that follows?

Word List 7: Answer Table

Word	Pronunciation	Part of Speech	Possible Meaning
gestation	jes-TAY-shun	noun	time in the uterus
prosthesis	pros-THEE-sis	noun	artificial body part
coroner	KOR-uhn-er	noun	medical examiner
manifest	MA-nuh-fest	verb	to make evident by showing or displaying
convalesce	kon-vuh-LESS	verb	to return to health after illness
recompense	re-KUHM-pents	noun	payment in return for something
immune	im-MYOON	adjective	protected from disease
debillitated	duh-BIL-i-tay-ted	adjective	tired and weak
Medicare	MED-i-kare	proper noun	a federal subsidy for care for the elderly
pandemic	pan-DEM-ik	adjective	widespread; epidemic over a large geographic region
quarantined	KWAHR-un-teend	adjective	isolated to protect the healthy
therapeutic	ther-ah-PYOO-tik	adjective	curative, rehabilitative
etiology	ee-tee-OL-uh-jcc	noun	study of the origin or cause of diseases
triage	TREE-ahj	noun	prioritization of victims for treatment
trauma	TRAH-muh	noun	sudden and serious medical condition

A Closer Look

Sound Clues

1. *j*, the *g* is followed by the letter *e*
2. *k*, the *c* is not followed by an *e*, *i*, or *y*
3. *k*, it is not followed by an *e*, *i*, or *y*
4. *s*, it is followed by an *e*
5. *j*, the *g* is followed by the letter *e*

Sight and Structure Clues

6. therapy
7. immunize or immunization
8. medical + care
9. pay back
10. the study of

Practice Exercises

Scrambled Letters

11. triage
12. coroner
13. trauma
14. pandemic
15. immune

True or False?

16. True
17. False
18. False
19. False
20. True

IN SHORT

In this lesson, you worked with words related to the field of healthcare, several of which were built on roots that gave you clues to their meaning. You'll find more medical and healthcare words in Lesson 8, where you'll see more examples of how root words can help you figure out unfamiliar words.

LESSON

8

WORD MEANING FROM ROOTS

In this lesson, as you encounter new words from the fields of medicine and healthcare, you will continue to explore more word roots that give clues to their meaning. Armed with a knowledge of many roots, you'll be able to continue to expand your vocabulary in the lessons that follow.

L ike plants, words also have roots from which they grow. Dig down into a new word, and most likely, you'll be able to unearth its meaning by examining its root. You've become familiar with many such roots now, and here you'll see more, as you become more and more aware of word structure.

WORD LIST 8

Below are sentences with this lesson's words in bold. As before, here's what you do:

- Read all the sentences.
- Underline bold words you already know and can define by sight.
- Put a star over bold words that seem familiar but that you cannot define by sight.
- Circle words in bold that are unfamiliar to you.

Sentences

The **prognosis** for her **malady**, simple fatigue, implied that recovery would be quick and successful.

The **neonatologist** was called to consult on the condition of the newborn baby who had breathing problems.

Poor **ventilation** can cause headaches and fatigue because it interrupts the body's heat-regulating mechanism.

The surgeon cut with her scalpel and made the **incision** directly above the knee.

The **toxicology** report showed that there were high levels of alcohol in the blood of the accident victim.

The **audiologist** said that his hearing had been damaged by high noise levels on his job.

The woman signed a healthcare **proxy** to allow her family to make her medical decisions when she could no longer make them for herself.

proxy

Before the body could be taken to the **morgue**, the **forensic** lab took many tissue samples for analysis.

morgue

In the table on the next page, each word's root has been indicated. Think about other words you know or recognize by sight that share those roots.

A CLOSER LOOK
The Meaning of Roots

Most of the roots in these words come from the ancient languages of Latin and Greek, although as you will see from time to time, words have roots from other languages as well. Each word root has a basic meaning that was developed in that root's original language, and this meaning has been carried over into English words as they evolved over the years. (Notice that the word *evolved* contains the Latin root *vol*, which means "to roll." You see this root in words such as *revolve* and *volume*— a word still used to refer to books, because books were originally written on scrolls that were rolled.)

Word List 8: Practice Table

Word	Root Meaning	Words That Share the Root	Word Meaning
pro**gno**sis	to know	*diagnose*, to judge the nature of a medical condition by signs or symptoms displayed	a prediction of the course of an illness
malady	bad	*malign*, to speak badly of someone	a bad condition
neo**nat**ologist	birth	*native*, where you were born	a doctor who deals with the diseases and care of newborns (*neo* means "new")
ventilation	wind		
in**cis**ion	cut		
toxicology	poison		
audiologist	hear		
proxy	near		
morgue	death		
forensic	public		

Here are some meanings behind the roots in the words from this lesson.

- pro**gno**sis: the root is *gno*, which comes from the Greek word meaning "to know." Sometimes, you see this root as *cogn*. From this root, we get words like *recognize* and *incognito*, both of which have to do with knowing the identity of someone.

- *mal*ady: the root is *mal*, which means "bad" or "ill" in the original Latin. This is a very common root that appears in many words having to do with something bad or unpleasant. For example:

  malice—bad feelings toward someone

  malignancy—a cancer (clearly, a bad diagnosis)

- neo*nat*ologist: the root *nat* comes from the Latin word for "birth." From this root, we get a number of words that have to do with birth:

  prenatal—before birth

  nativity—birth

- *vent*ilation: the root *vent* in this word means "wind." From this root, we get words such as:

  ventifact—a stone worn or polished by windblown sand

  vent—to expose to air

- in*cis*ion: this word contains the root *cis*, which means "to cut." From this root, we get words such as:

  scissors—cutting device with sharp edges

  precise—clear and exact (as in "closely cut")

- *toxi*cology: the root *toxi* means "poison." We see this root in these words:

  intoxicated—poisoned by alcohol

  toxic—poisonous

- *aud*iologist: the root *aud* means "to hear." We see this root in many words having to do with hearing or being heard:

  audience—a group that hears a performance

  audition—performance heard by an evaluator, such as a potential employer or a casting director

- *prox*y: the root here is *prox*, which means "near." We see this root in words such as:

  approximation—a close guess

  proximity—nearness

- *mor*gue: the root here is *mor* from *mort*, meaning "death." Words that share this root include:

  mortician—one who prepares a body for burial

  mortuary—a place where the dead are prepared for burial

- *for*ensic: the root here comes from the Latin word *forum*, which means "a public place." The word forensic refers to information that can be made public or can bring about a public good. For example:

  forensic science—the science that analyzes information that may be helpful to the public by helping to solve a crime

  forensics—the practice of public debate

Extending the Roots

Match the words in column A with their meanings in column B by considering the meaning of the roots in bold.

	A		B
1.	_____ *mal*nutrition	**a.**	place where performances are heard
2.	_____ in*toxi*cate	**b.**	undying
3.	_____ im*mort*al	**c.**	condition brought about by a bad diet
4.	_____ con*cise*	**d.**	to poison by alcohol
5.	_____ *audi*torium	**e.**	clear cut; brief

Sight Cues

Reading quickly, circle the words that appear in this lesson.

6. notation / neoclassical / neologism / neonatologist

7. ventricle / ventilator / ventilation / ventifact

8. foreign / foresight / forensics / forehand

9. indecision / incisive / instinct / incision

10. mortal / morgue / moral / morphine

Meanings for Word List 8

Here are the words for this lesson, with their pronunciations and definitions.

prognosis (prahg-NOE-sis) : a prediction of the probable course and result of a disease

malady (MAL-uh-dee): a condition of illness; an ailment

neonatologist (neeoh-nay-TAHL-ujee) a doctor who deals with the diseases and care of newborn infants

ventilation (ven-tuhl-AY-shun): the replacement of stale or noxious air with clean, fresh air; the mechanical system used to do this

incision (in-SI-zhun): a gash or cut, as in a surgical cut

toxicology (tocks-i-KOL-uh-jee): the study of poisons

audiologist (aw-dee-OL-uh-jist): one who treats hearing problems

proxy (PROCK-see): a person authorized to act in the place of another

morgue (MORG): a place where dead bodies are kept until burial

forensic (for-EN-zik): pertaining to information used in a court of law

PRACTICE EXERCISES

Test your knowledge of the words in Word List 8.

The Right Word

Choose the correct word or words in each sentence.

11. Her (prognosis / diagnosis) for recovery was a good one.

12. One who suffers an ailment has a (malady / malefactor).

13. If you had a hearing problem, you would consult an (audiologist / audition).

14. When cooking on the stove, it is important to have proper (respiration / ventilation) so that the fumes don't accumulate.

15. A neonatologist takes care of (newborn babies / babies who've had their first birthdays).

Missing Letters

Fill in the missing letters in the words.

16. t__ __icology

17. mor__ __e

18. pr__ __y

19. f__ __ensic

20. in__ __ __ion

ANSWERS

Here are some ways you could use the approaches for two of this lesson's words:

Morgue—unless you know the root *mor*, you would probably need the context to signal the meaning here.

Proxy sounds like *approximately*.

Check the table you filled in against the completed sample table that follows. You may have thought of some different words to fill in than the ones given here.

Word List 8: Answer Table

Word	Root Meaning	Words That Share the Root	Word Meaning
pro*gno*sis	to know	*diagnose*, to judge the nature of a medical condition by signs or symptoms displayed	a prediction of the course of an illness
*mal*ady	bad	*malign*, to speak badly of someone	a bad condition
neo*nat*ologist	birth	*native*, where you were born	a doctor who deals with the diseases and care of newborns (*neo* means "new")
*vent*ilation	wind	*ventifact*, a stone worn or polished by wind-blown sand	the replacement of stale or noxious air with clean fresh air
in*cis*ion	cut	*incisor*, a cutting tooth	a cut
*toxic*ology	poison	*toxic*, poisonous	the study of poisons
*audi*ologist	hear	*audiotape*, a means of recording sound	doctor of hearing
*prox*y	near	*proximity*, closeness	authorization to act for someone
*mor*gue	death	*mortal*, susceptible to dying	place where the dead are kept
*for*ensic	public	*forum*, a public place	pertaining to information used in court

A Closer Look

Extending the Roots

1. c

2. d

3. b

4. e

5. a

Sight Cues

6. neonatologist

7. ventilation

8. forensics

9. incision

10. morgue

Practice Exercises

The Right Word

11. prognosis

12. malady

13. audiologist

14. ventilation

15. newborn babies

Missing Letters

16. to*x*icology

17. mor*gu*e

18. pr*ox*y

19. fo*r*ensic

20. in*cis*ion

IN SHORT

Now you've got more roots to add to your root word list, and all these roots grow into many more words. In the next lesson, you will look at more root words.

LESSON

9

WORDS FROM BUSINESS AND FINANCE

The words in this lesson are drawn from the employment world. These include common business terms and words related to the fields of finance and marketing, as well as terms that could be heard around the coffeepot at almost anyone's job.

Pick up a newspaper, a general news magazine, or a union newsletter, and you'll come across some of the words in this lesson. Even if you don't work in business or finance, knowing these words will help you better understand business and economic matters that, in one way or another, affect us all.

WORD LIST 9

Each of the following sentences contains one or more of this lesson's words. You know what to do:

- Read all the sentences.
- Underline bold words you already know and can define by sight.
- Put a star over bold words that seem familiar but that you cannot define by sight.
- Circle words in bold that are unfamiliar to you.

Sentences

The job offered an excellent **401(k)** plan after just three months of employment.

The government can **levy** a private citizen's taxes to assess how much is owed.

import

One can make a lot of money **importing** goods from other countries and selling them here.

merger

The **merger** of several large lending institutions has meant that by joining together, they have even greater power over the marketplace.

Businesses and individuals hire **portfolio** managers to keep track of their mix of investments and expenditures, including a strict accounting of any **capital** that is gained or lost.

The students were disappointed when their favorite professor was denied **tenure** by her department and had to leave her position at the university.

In recent years, **franchises**, such as fast food chains, muffler shops, and footwear stores, have become a rapidly growing form of business.

The Internet offers enormous opportunities for **entrepreneurs** who are willing to take a risk on an untried business.

entitlement

Lawmakers are reluctant to cut so-called **entitlement** programs such as Medicare and Medicaid from the budget.

The oil **cartel** of countries in the Middle East has grown less powerful in recent years.

One of the disputed issues between labor and management to be resolved in **arbitration** is that of the use of **per diem** workers in place of full-time workers. Although union leaders agreed to management's proposal, the **rank and file** rejected it.

In the seventeenth and eighteenth centuries, the **bourgeois** attitude opposed the privileges held by nobles.

Take each of the bold words in the sentences you just read and fill in the table on the next page, using the first three samples as your guide.

A CLOSER LOOK
Roots in Words

Think back to Lesson 8, when you were introduced to word roots. There are more word roots here to help you with some of the word meanings you're focusing on in this lesson.

Root Exercises

The word *portfolio* contains two roots that contribute to its meaning: The root *port* means "to carry," and the root *fol* means "leaf." Originally, the word *portfolio* meant "a sheaf of papers," like leaves in a book that could be carried in a folder. Now we refer to a flat carrying case for papers as a "portfolio." The word also means "a list of investments owned by a person or a business." Your *portfolio* represents your worth in the market.

Fill in the root in the related words that follow.

    port—to carry

1. Something you can carry easily is __ __ __ __able.

2. Something that carries you to where you want to go—a car, bus, train, or plane—is a means of trans__ __ __ __ation.

3. Goods brought into of a country are called im__ __ __ __ __.

    folio—leaf

4. In October, we enjoy the sight of the beautiful fall __ __ __iage.

5. Chemicals are used to de__ __ __iate trees in wartime.

6. The chemical compound __ __ __ic acid is used to treat anemia.

Word List 9: Practice Table

Word	Pronunciation	Meaning
401(k)	fore-oh-wun-KAYE	a tax-deferred retirement investment account
levy	LE-ve	to impose an assessment or a tax
import	IM-port	goods brought in from their original countries for trade or sale
merger		
portfolio		
capital		
tenure		
franchise		
entrepreneur		
entitlement		
cartel		
arbitration		
per diem		
rank and file		
bourgeois		

The word *capital* derives from the Latin root *cap*, which means "head." Some-times, this root extends to words that mean chief, first, or ultimate, as in *capital punishment*—the most severe form of justice. *Capital* can also refer to the money or property owned by a business.

Fill in the root in the related words.

7. __ __ __italism is the system of economics based on private ownership and for-profit operation.

8. A __ __ __ital letter is the first letter in a sentence.

The word *tenure* derives from the root *ten*, which means "to hold." An employee with tenure literally "holds onto" a job for life. The *ten* root appears in a number of other words with similar meanings.

Fill in the root to make other words you might want to know.

9. He had the __ __ __acity to hold to his opinion despite much opposition.

10. He was in an un__ __ __able position that was difficult to hold to under current circumstances.

Foreign Words

From the clues given in the sentences for Word List 9 near the start of this lesson, choose the word that matches the meanings.

11. A word derived from a French word that means "business"

_____

12. A word derived from a French word that means "citizen of a town"

_____

13. A word derived from the Latin that means "by the day"

_____

Meanings for Word List 9

Here are the pronunciations and meanings for the words in this lesson. How many did you know?

401(k) (fore-oh-wun-KAYE): a retirement investment account that allows an employee to save money tax-deferred

levy (LE-vee): impose an assessment, such as a tax

import (IM-port): to bring in goods from another country for the purpose of trade or sale

merger (MUR-jur): a combining of two or more businesses into one

portfolio (port-FOH-lee-oh): the group of investments being held at any one time by an investor. It can also mean a flat, notebook-size folder for carrying important papers

capital (KAP-it-ul): the money or property owned by or invested in a business. It also can describe the first letter in a sentence

tenure (TEN-yoor): the state or period of holding a particular job. For teachers, it is a guarantee of employment after meeting certain standards of performance

franchise (FRAN-chyze): can refer to a license to sell a particular product or service (e.g., hamburgers, brake jobs, or pet supplies) in a business that is individually owned and operated

entrepreneur (ahn-truh-pre-NOOR): a person who starts up and usually manages a new business

entitlement (en-TEYTE-ul-muhnt): special privileges or benefits to a particular group of people. The adjective describes government programs that offer special benefits to a group of citizens; examples of such programs include Social Security, Medicare, and Medicaid

cartel (kar-TEL): the union of a group of businesses that have joined together for the purpose of controlling an industry

arbitration (ahr-bi-TRAY-shun): the settling of disputes by a third party who has no stake in either side

per diem (pur DEE-um): by the day, as in per diem workers, who are hired by the day instead of on a long-term contract

rank and file (RANK and FYLE): general membership in a labor union.

bourgeois (BOO-zhwah): a characteristic marked by a concern for material pursuits and industrial interests

PRACTICE EXERCISES

Test your memory of the words in this lesson.

Fill in the Blanks

Fill in the correct words in the following sentences.

14. The _____ between the companies failed because the executive officers could not agree on how to share the profits.

15. The strip mall outside of town had a number of fast-food restaurants and other _____ operations.

16. The international oil _____ was responsible for driving up the price of oil in the 1980s.

17. The agency _____ a fine against him for not paying back the money he owed.

18. The _____ are the general members of a labor union.

True or False?

Mark the following statements as True or False, according to the meaning of the indicated words.

19. _____ Most countries try to export more goods than they *import*.

20. _____ An *entitlement* program offers a promotion to top executives.

21. _____ Working on a *per diem* basis means that you work for half a day or less.

22. _____ A *401(k)* plan earns money for retirement benefits.

23. _____ High *levies* on goods imported to the United States protect American products.

24. _____ A *bourgeois* attitude is concerned with material interests.

ANSWERS

Using the four approaches, here are some ways to find clues about the meaning of some of the words in Word List 9.

Merger looks like the word *merge.*

Entitlement sounds like a familiar word, *entitled.*

Import has a structure clue: *-port* ("to carry")

Check the table you filled in against the sample table that follows.

Word List 9: Answer Table

Word	Pronunciation	Meaning
401(k)	fore-oh-wun-KAYE	a tax-deferred retirement invetstment account
levy	LE-ve	to impose an assessment or a tax
import	IM-port	to bring goods in from their original countries for trade or sale
merger	MUR-jur	companies joining together
portfolio	port-FOH-lee-oh	a list of current investments
capital	KAP-it-ul	money invested in a business
tenure	TEN-yoor	permanent employment, or total amount of time someone remains in a position
franchise	FRAN-chyze	a chain of businesses, such as fast-food restaurants or coffeeshops
entrepreneur	ahn-truh-pre-NOOR	organizer and manager of a business
entitlement	en-TYTE-uhl-muhnt	Medicare and Medicaid and other such government aid programs
cartel	kar-TEL	groups of businesses that combine to control markets
arbitration	ahr-bi-TRAY-shun	negotiating an agreement with an independent third person
per diem	pur DEE-um	by the day; per day
rank and file	RANK and FYLE	ordinary union members
bourgeois	BOO-zwah	marked by concern for material interests

A Closer Look
Root Exercises
1. *port*able
2. trans*port*ation
3. im*port*s
4. *fol*iage
5. de*fol*iate
6. *fol*ic acid
7. *cap*italism
8. *cap*ital
9. *ten*acity
10. un*ten*able

Foreign Words
11. entrepreneur
12. bourgeois
13. per diem

Practice Exercises
Fill in the Blanks
14. merger
15. franchise
16. cartel
17. levied
18. rank and file

True or False?
19. False
20. False
21. False
22. True
23. True
24. True

IN SHORT

In this lesson, you were introduced to words from the business world. You may have noticed that a number of these words have parts that remind you of other words that you already know. It is that recognition that helps you link what you already know with what appears to be new or unfamiliar.

LESSON

10

WORD MEANING FROM PREFIXES

In this lesson, you will learn how prefixes can alter or change the meaning of a word—and how the recognition of common ones can unlock the meaning of many words for you.

Being familiar with the meaning of the most frequently used prefixes can help you add to your reading, speaking, and listening vocabularies. This lesson focuses on prefixes in words that are drawn from the worlds of business and finance. You'll see how a relatively short list of prefixes can give you access to many new and interesting words.

STARTING WITH PREFIXES

Let's begin with one root, *spec*, meaning "to look," along with several prefixes that alter the meaning of the word in which *spec* appears.

Prefix	+ Root	= New Word	Example
in (upon)	*spect*	*inspect:* to look into	The officer will *inspect* the luggage.
circum (around)	*spect*	*circumspect:* cautious, looking around	They were *circumspect* in their questions to the suspect.
intro (before)	*spect*	*introspection:* looking inward	He was given to *introspection,* seriously considering his plans for the future
retro (back)	*spect*	*retrospect:* looking backward	In *retrospect*, I would have acted differently.
pro (forward)	*spect*	*prospect:* a look forward	I enjoyed the *prospect* of a vacation on Cape Cod this year.

Numerical Prefixes

Probably among the most easily recognized of the prefixes are the numerical prefixes; that is, those that tell something about the number represented by the word. You've already seen some words that contain numerical prefixes: *bipartisan* (two parties), *triage* (responding to needs in order of priority, traditionally in three orders of priority), and *trilogy* (a series of three plays). Among the common number-related prefixes are:

- *un, mono*—one (unique, monotonous, unity, monopoly)
- *bi*—two (bigamy, bilateral, bicameral, bicycle)
- *tri*—three (trivial, trident, trinity, triple)
- *quad, quar*—four (quadrant, quarter, quart, quartet)
- *deci*—ten (decade, decathlon, decimal, decibel)
- *cent*—hundred (century, centipede, centennial)
- *mil*—thousand (millipede, millenium, millimeter)

Prefixes Change Words

The point of learning about prefixes is to be able to notice how they can change word meanings in recognizable ways. Some prefixes immediately change the entire meaning of a word. For example, the prefixes *un-*, *in-*, *dis-*, and *il-* immediately signal that the word is the opposite of its root, as in **un**happy, **in**considerate, **dis**pleasing, and **il**legible.

Other prefixes only remotely affect word meaning. For example, there is only a distant hint of the prefix *deci-*, which means "ten," in the word *decimate*, which means "to completely destroy." Historically, the word *decimate* meant to destroy a large part, perhaps a tenth, of someone's property. Now we hardly recognize that meaning in the present definition.

The important point to remember is that in learning prefixes, you are not looking to memorize a long list of disconnected word parts, but to recognize familiar examples that you can apply to new words when you meet them.

WORD LIST 10

On the next page are some sentences that contain additional words from the fields of business and finance. Each contains a prefix that acts on the root word to change or enhance its meaning.

You know what to do:

- Read all the sentences.
- Underline bold words you already know and can define by sight.
- Put a star over bold words that seem familiar but that you cannot define by sight.
- Circle words in bold that are unfamiliar to you.

Sentences

In an effort to reach out to all races, many companies promote a **multicultural** environment by recruiting employees that speak more than one language.

Medical **benefits** are available to most full-time employees in jobs that offer health insurance.

Many small companies rely on **telemarketing** to reach a wide range of customers.

In some companies, getting **promoted** is automatic after a designated amount of time.

There have been widespread fears that one large computer company would create such a **monopoly** that smaller competitors would be driven out of business.

The **recession** slowed the economy and created the largest unemployment rate in many years.

After getting laid off for a second time this year, he was so **demoralized** that he didn't want to go on any more job interviews.

A high school diploma is a **prerequisite** for most jobs in government or law enforcement.

There is a need for private industry as well as government to **subsidize** job opportunities for persons entering the workforce for the first time.

The worker received **compensation** for his injury on the job.

Complete the following table based on your recognition of familiar prefixes. You will need to guess at word meanings by trying to think about other words that you already know that share that prefix.

Word List 10: Practice Table

Word	Pronunciation	Other Words That Use These Word Parts	Possible Meaning
multicultural	mul-tee-KUHL-chur-uhl	*multiply*, make many of	of or referring to many cultures
benefits	BEN-uh-fits	*benediction*, a good word pronounced on something	something good
telemarketing	TEL-e-MAHR-ket-ing	*telephone*, hearing at a distance	selling at a distance
promote			
monopoly			
recession			
demoralize			
prerequisite			
subsidize			
compensation			

A CLOSER LOOK
Prefixes

Look at the following list of prefixes. Then choose from these prefixes to make new words in the blanks in the sentences that follow.

- *re*: back or away from; again
- *com*: with or together
- *pro*: forward; ahead
- *pre*: before
- *mono*: one
- *multi*: many
- *sub*: under
- *inter*: between
- *tele*: at a distance
- *contra*: against

1. If you state something that is against or the opposite of what someone else said, your point stands in __ __ __ __ __ __diction to their view.

2. A(n) __ __ __ __ __im appointment comes between two people serving on a job.

3. If you speak in only one tone of voice, your speech becomes __ __ __ __tonous.

4. A(n) __ __ __nuptial agreement takes place before marriage.

Prefixes and Roots

Here is another example of how a single root can make many words by adding different prefixes. Combine the prefixes and the root to make new words. Then choose one of the new words you have made to fill in the blanks in the sentences that follow.

ject—a root form that means "to throw"

Prefix	+	Root	=	New Word	
in	+	ject		_____	("to throw in")
pro	+	ject		_____	("to throw forward")
re	+	ject		_____	("to throw back")
inter	+	ject		_____	("to throw between")

5. He _____(ed) her appeal for more money.

6. The _____(or) threw the moving images on the screen.

7. He refused to _____ himself into the argument.

8. He _____(ed) a note of humor into the dismal reading of the will.

Meanings for Word List 10

Here are the words from this lesson with pronunciations and meanings. Included are other words that share the same root.

multicultural (mul-tee-KUHL-chur-uhl): relating to or including several cultures. (Other words with same root: *multi*lingual, *multi*color, *multi*million.)

benefits (BEN-uh-fits): medical and other insurance coverage given to employees as part of their contract to work. (Other words with same root: *bene*ficial, *beni*gn, *bene*diction.)

telemarketing (TEL-e-MAHR-ket-ing): outreach to potential customers by means of telephone solicitation. (Other words with same root: *tele*pathy, *tele*vision, *tele*phone.)

promote (pruh-MOTE): to raise to a more responsible rank or job. (Other words with same root: *pro*fessional, *pro*active, *pro*create.)

monopoly (mon-OP-uh-lee): control of a market by a single business. (Other words with same root: *mono*graph, *mono*rail, *mono*lith, *mono*tone.)

recession (ree-CESS-shun): a periodic falling off of business activity. (Other words with same root: *re*press, *re*unite, *re*lapse.)

demoralize (dee-MOHR-uh-lize): to undermine the confidence or morale of. (Other words with same root: *de*value, *de*classify, *de*certify.)

prerequisite (pree-REK-wi-zit): something required before beginning a course, job, or activity (noun); required before beginning (adjective). (Other words with same root: *pre*cursor, *pre*liminary, *pre*ordained.)

subsidize (SUB-si-dyze): to support financially a group or institution that cannot manage independently. (Other words with same root: *sub*contract, *sub*poena, *sub*sistence.)

compensation (kom-pen-SAY-shun): payment for services rendered. Sometimes, compensation attempts to redress injuries or bad experiences on a job. (Other words with same root: *com*prehend, *com*panion, *com*pile.)

PRACTICE EXERCISES

How well do you know the words in this lesson?

Matching

Team the word in column A with its meaning in column B.

A	B
9. subsidize	**a.** a temporary slowdown in the economy
10. benefits	**b.** control of an industry by a single company
11. demoralize	**c.** give financial support
12. monopoly	**d.** to undermine the confidence of
13. recession	**e.** insurance from employers.

Fill in the Blanks

Complete the spelling of the words by filling in the missing letters.

14. tele__ __ __keting

15. pre__ __ __ __ __site

16. com__ __ __sation

17. __ __ __ __ __cultural

18. pro__ __ __ __ed

ANSWERS

Word List 10: Answer Table

Word	Pronunciation	Other Words That Use These Word Parts	Possible Meaning
multicultural	mul-tee-KUHL-chur-uhl	*multiply*, make many of	of or referring to many cultures
benefits	BEN-uh-fits	*benediction*, a good word pronounced on something	something good
telemarketing	TEL-e-MAHR-ket-ing	*telephone*, hearing at a distance	selling at a distance

promote	pruh-MOTE	*proceed*, to go before	to raise to a more responsible rank or job
monopoly	mon-OP-uh-lee	*monogram*, a single letter	control by one company
recession	ree-CESS-shun	*recall*, call back	going back
demoralize	dee-MOHR-uh-lize	*demote*, to assign a job of lesser rank	to undermine the confidence or morale of
prerequisite	pree-REK-wi-zit	*prenatal*, before birth	something required before
subsidize	SUB-si-dyze	*submarine*, underwater	underwrite, give money or support
compensation	kom-pen-SAY-shun	*companion*, someone with you	money for injury

A Closer Look

Prefixes
1. *contra*diction
2. *inter*im
3. *mono*tonous
4. *pre*nuptial

Prefixes and Roots
5. inject
6. projector
7. rejected
8. interjected

Practice Exercises

Matching
9. c
10. e
11. d
12. b
13. a

Fill in the Blanks
14. tele*mar*keting
15. pre*requi*site
16. com*pen*sation
17. *multi*cultural
18. pro*ject*ed

IN SHORT

In this lesson, you learned to look at the beginnings of words, or their prefixes, to get a clue to their meanings. Prefixes often change the meanings of the base or root words. Be alert to the common numerical and other prefixes and you will see how words change when a prefix is added to them.

LESSON

11

WORDS FROM NAMES

In this lesson, you will meet words that are derived from the names of real and fictitious people, places, and events. These names are called *eponyms*.

In Lesson 5, you were introduced to many scientific and technical words that were brought into English from other languages. Similarly, English has incorporated many names of people and places from world and American history, from literature (especially mythology), and from popular culture. In many cases, as you'll see in this lesson, English has adapted these proper names into the common names of the things associated with their origin.

The *frisbee*, a game that uses a plastic disk, took its definition from Mrs. Frisbee's Pies, a Connecticut bakery. The metal pie plates from those frozen pies had been used for years by students who tossed them to each other on the local school campus.

The *cardigan* sweater took its name from Lord Cardigan, a nineteenth-century Englishman who popularized the open-fronted jacket.

The *tuxedo* came from the wealthy suburban community of Tuxedo, New York, where the tail-less dress suit was first worn by male members of high society.

The *sandwich* gets its name from the Earl of Sandwich, who, it is said, put his meat between two pieces of bread so that he could hold his lunch in one hand and his playing cards in the other.

Recognizing, remembering, and using words like these can add a colorful dimension to your reading, speaking, and listening vocabularies.

WORD LIST 11

Here are some words that have come to the English language from proper names. As usual:

- Read all the sentences.
- Underline bold words you already know and can define by sight
- Put a star over bold words that seem familiar but that you cannot define by sight.
- Circle words in bold that are unfamiliar to you.

Sentences

I'm so **lethargic** when I first get up that I need two cups of coffee to get me moving.

Karate and judo, two of the **martial** arts, place a strong emphasis on body control and ritual.

Unfortunately, these earrings are **rhinestones**, not diamonds.

The jeans were made of heavy blue **denim**.

My aunt, who's so **jovial**, is always a happy and outgoing hostess.

Proper **hygiene**, such as brushing your teeth, is something that should be practiced daily.

Nobody would argue that **nicotine** is not a cancer-causing agent.

A **silhouette** that I drew of my cat is my favorite piece of artwork.

She was a real **maverick** who never wanted to do what the other girls in her group agreed to.

Their **platonic** relationship was built not upon passion but on mutual respect and many shared experiences over the years.

The teacher returned to find a classroom in **bedlam**; the students were having a loud, wild time throwing pencils and papers everywhere.

I can rarely get my **laconic** neighbor to chat with me over the fence.

The **quixotic** candidate ran on a campaign for "better everything"!

quixotic

The fool in the play continually mixed up his words, which resulted in ridiculous **malapropisms** that had the audience in fits of laughter.

malapropism

He put forth a **herculean** effort to save the two toddlers from the raging river.

On the basis of the usage of the words in the sentences you just read, fill in the information missing from the table.

Word List 11: Practice Table

Word	Pronunciation	Part of Speech
lethargic	leth-AHR-jik	adjective
martial	MAHR-shul	adjective
rhinestone	RINE-stone	
denim	DEN-um	
jovial	JOH-vee-ul	
hygiene	HEYE-jeen	
nicotine	NIK-uh-teen	
silhouette	sil-oo-ET	
maverick	MAV-uh-rik	
platonic	pluh-TON-ik	
bedlam	BED-luhm	
laconic	luh-KON-ik	
quixotic	kwik-SOT-ik	
malapropism	MAL-uh-prop-izum	
herculean	her-kyoo-LEE-un	

A CLOSER LOOK

At the beginning of this lesson, you met a few eponyms that have worked their way into English. Here are the ones from Word List 11, with their meanings and origins.

A **lethargic** person is sleepy and sluggish in his movements. The word comes from the name of the river Lethe in Greek mythology, which was the river of forgetfulness.

The **martial** arts are a form of ritualized combat. The word comes from the Greek god Mars, the deity of war.

The "rhine" in **rhinestone** refers the Rhine River in France. The word *rhinestone* is a translation of the French phrase *caillou du Rhin*, which means "pebble of the Rhine." Originally, a rhinestone was a kind of rock crystal that was found in or near the Rhine. Because it was found that rhinestones could be made to imitate diamonds, the name *rhinestone* was used to describe artificial gems made from paste, glass, or gem quartz.

The name for **denim** fabric for blue jeans is derived from the French term *serge de Nimes*, from the city of Nimes (pronounced Neem) where the material originated.

A **jovial** person is sociable and outgoing. The word comes from the Greek god Jove, the spirit of revelry and celebration.

The word **hygiene**, which refers to the promotion of good health, is named after the Greek goddess of health, Hygeia.

Jean Nicot, a French diplomat, introduced the tobacco plant to France in approximately 1561. Thus, tobacco was named **nicotine** on his behalf.

The word **silhouette** is named after Etienne de Silhouette, the finance minister of France under Louis XV, who was known for his amateurish portraits.

A **maverick** is a rebel or dissenter, a free thinker who doesn't follow party leadership. The word comes from the name of a rancher who refused to brand his animals for identification. A person who doesn't conform to institutional policy is a maverick.

Relationships that are **platonic** do not involve physical attraction. The word comes from the name of the philosopher Plato, who taught that people could relate to each other on an intellectual level alone.

The word **bedlam** is used to refer to a place or condition of noisy confusion. It is derived from the name of Bethlehem Hospital in London, which was an asylum for the criminally insane. It survives as a word used to describe any loud, chaotic atmosphere, such as a school lunchroom or the winning locker room after a big game.

A **laconic** person is someone who speaks briefly and concisely. The word comes from the people of ancient Laconia, who were said to be people of few words. We often see this word used to describe independent types such as cowboys who say as little as possible.

A **quixotic** person is an impractical idealist. The term comes from the literary character Don Quixote, an elderly scholar who pursues imaginary quests thinking he is a knight from the Age of Chivalry.

A **malapropism** is a humorous misuse of the language. For example, when the character Archie Bunker from the 1970s television sitcom *All in the Family* says, "I'm not prejudiced. That's a pigment of your imagination," his confusion of *figment* with *pigment* and its association with skin color is amusing. The term comes from the name of the character Mrs. Malaprop in Sheridan's eighteenth-century play *The Rivals*. She was known for frequently making similarly comic misstatements.

A **herculean** effort is often required to accomplish great deeds. The word comes from the name of the mythological hero Hercules, who performed incredible labors to prove his strength.

Word Origins

Fill in the blanks in the following sentences.

1. Five words that come to English from Greek and Roman mythology are

_____, _____,

_____, _____, and

_____.

2. Four words that come to English from the names of places are

_____, _____,

_____, and _____.

3. Two words that come into English from the names of literary

characters are _____ and _____.

Phonetics

On the basis of the pronunciations given in Word List 11, answer the following:

4. Three words in which the letter *c* carries the *k* sound in the middle of the

word are _____, _____, and

_____.

5. A word that has the long *e* sound, but contains no letter *e*, is

_____.

6. A word in which the letter *y* represents a long *i* sound is

_____.

7. A word that changed in its form and pronunciation when it evolved into

current usage is _____.

Meanings for Word List 11

This box shows the words in this lesson, with their pronunciations and meanings. How many did you get right?

lethargic (leth-AHR-jik): sleepy, sluggish

martial (MAHR-shul): warlike, hostile

rhinestone (RINE-stone): a colorless artificial gem of paste or glass

denim (DEN-um): a kind of heavy work fabric

jovial (JOH-vee-ul): pleasant, good-tempered

hygiene (HEYE-jeen): practices that promote good health

nicotine (NIK-uh-teen): a colorless, poisonous alkaloid that is derived from the tobacco plant; the substance to which tobacco smokers can become addicted

silhouette (sil-oo-ET): a drawing of an outline of something, such as a human profile

maverick (MAV-uh-RIK): a rebel or dissenter (noun); rebellious or dissenting (adjective)

platonic (pluh-TON-ik): not involving physical attraction; intellectual

bedlam (BED-luhm): a place or condition of noise and confusion

laconic (luh-KON-ik): brief in speech; uncommunicative

quixotic (kwik-SOT-ik): foolishly idealistic

malapropism (MAL-uh-prop-izum): a humorous misuse of the language

herculean (her-kyoo-LEE-un): massive or intense, as an effort to complete a large task

PRACTICE EXERCISES

Test your mastery of Word List 11.

True or False?

Answer True or False to the following sentences, on the basis of your knowledge of the meanings of the words in this lesson.

8. _____ A jovial, outgoing person would probably be *laconic* in his speech.

9. _____ Diamonds are not as valuable as *rhinestones*, which can be sewn onto *denim* clothing for decorative purposes.

10. _____ Practicing good *hygiene* is important in maintaining good health.

11. _____ For most, the *nicotine* in tobacco is so addictive that quitting smoking requires a *herculean* effort.

12. _____ A *lethargic* person would be interested in the *martial* arts.

Fill in the Blanks

Complete the words that appear in the sentences below.

13. Romeo and Juliet wanted more than a(n) __ __ __ __ __nic relationship. (*Clue:* named for a Greek philosopher.)

14. A sil __ __ __ __ __ te is a drawing of an outline of something, such as a human profile.

15. A m__ __ __ __ __ __k is a person who refuses to do the conventional thing.

(*Clue:* named for a rancher who refused to brand his livestock.)

16. The media circus that attends highly publicized events creates a

b__ __ __ __ m that can be annoying to mere observers.

(*Clue:* derived from the name of a London hospital for the insane.)

17. "Our relationship is strictly plutonic" is an example of a

__ __ __ __ __ __ __ __ism, a humorous misuse or confusion of words.

(*Clue:* named for a character in a Sheridan play who uses inappropriate words.)

Spelling Check

Circle the word in each group that is spelled correctly.

18. bedllum / bedlame / bedlim / bedlam

19. laconick / lanocik / laconic / laconec

20. niccotine / nicoteen / nicotine / nikotine

21. marshal / martail / martial / marteal

22. hurculean / herculaen / hercluean / herculean

ANSWERS

Here are clues to some of the words in this lesson:

Malapropism has two structural clues in it. The prefix *mal-* means "bad," and *apropos* is the French form of the word *appropriate*. Malapropisms are inappropriate usages.

Quixotic may have a visual clue; because so few familiar words contain *quix-*, you might well recognize the name of a well-known literary character.

Word List 11: Answer Table

Word	Pronunciation	Part of Speech
lethargic	leth-AHR-jik	adjective
martial	MAHR-shul	adjective
rhinestone	RINE-stone	noun
denim	DEN-um	adjective
jovial	JOH-vee-ul	adjective
hygiene	HEYE-jeen	noun
nicotine	NIK-uh-teen	noun
silhouette	sil-oo-ET	noun
maverick	MAV-uh-rik	noun or adjective
platonic	pluh-TON-ik	adjective
bedlam	BED-luhm	noun
laconic	luh-KON-ik	adjective
quixotic	kwik-SOT-ik	adjective
malapropism	MAL-uh-prop-izum	noun
herculean	her-kyoo-LEE-un	adjective

A Closer Look

Word Origins

1. lethargic, martial, herculean, hygiene, jovial
2. bedlam, denim, laconic, rhinestone
3. quixotic, malapropism

Phonetics

4. herculean, laconic, nicotine
5. jovial
6. hygiene
7. denim

Practice Exercises

True or False?

8. False
9. False
10. True
11. True
12. False

Spelling Check

18. bedlam
19. laconic
20. nicotine
21. martial
22. herculean

Fill in the Blanks

13. *plat*onic
14. sil*houet*te
15. m*averic*k
16. b*edla*m
17. *malaprop*ism

IN SHORT

In this lesson, you have encountered a number of words that are derived from names of people, places, and events. Eponyms like these show us how the language is constantly adding new and interesting forms of words from many different sources. In the next lesson, you will meet more of these interesting words and terms.

LESSON 12

WORD MEANING FROM SUFFIXES

Beginning with Lesson 2, you have been looking at how words are used in sentences and the parts of speech that identify their usage. In this lesson, you will look more closely at how words are changed according to the job they perform in the sentence. For many words, this change is made by their endings, called suffixes.

Like people who perform a number of tasks or jobs during the course of their daily lives, words, too, can do different things at different times. The suffix is an ending syllable that changes the function of a word without necessarily changing its meaning. For example, here is a word that has a different suffix for each kind of work it performs.

Specify: to mention or name exactly

- As a **verb**, it wears a past tense *-ed* ending: He *specified* that he wanted the small, red compact car.
- As a **noun**, it wears the *-tion* ending: His *specifications* were followed to the letter.
- As an **adjective**, it wears the *-ic* suffix: He had a *specific* car in mind when he placed the order.

- As an **adverb**, it wears the *-ly* ending: He *specifically* noted the color and model he wanted.

WORD LIST 12

First, you will meet some more words like those in Lesson 11 that are derived from proper names. Then, you'll see how they can be used differently, according to their suffixes. Later, you will see some additional suffixes that you may find in other words.

You know what to do:

- Read all the sentences.
- Underline bold words you already know and can define by sight.
- Put a star over bold words that seem familiar but that you cannot define by sight.
- Circle words in bold that are unfamiliar to you.

Sentences

narcissistic

He was so **narcissistic** that he would look at himself in every mirror he passed.

The critic's **cynicism** gave him a particularly negative view of the film.

Before **pasteurization**, people could become sick with typhoid fever from the microorganisms found in milk.

Townsfolk were so concerned about **vandalism** that they formed a neighborhood watch to prevent more destruction of property.

My editor **bowdlerized** my novel to such an extent that I no longer recognized it as my own.

They believed that a **utopian** society, where everyone was content and equal in every way, was possible.

The dreamlike quality of the music **mesmerized** the listeners.

He is so engrossed in the **academic** lifestyle that he is not aware of the outside world.

The well-trained soldier's **stoicism** in face of danger kept him from fleeing the battle.

Draconian measures were taken to keep the prisoners under control.

All of the highlighted words in the sentences you just read have other forms, some of which are made with the addition of a suffix. In the table on the next page, using your best guess, how might the words sound as they become different parts of speech?

A CLOSER LOOK
The Suffix *-ize*
The verb suffix *-ize* means "to bring about." For example:
- A performance may *mesmerize* or fascinate an audience. This word comes from the name of Franz Mesmer, a well-known hypnotist in France.
- To *pasteurize* milk means to destroy its harmful bacteria by heating it for a short period of time. The process is named after Louis Pasteur, the French scientist who discovered it in the 1800s.

The Suffix *-ist*
The noun suffix *-ist* means "one who is." For example:
- A *narcissist* is someone who is self-absorbed or conceited. The word comes from the name of a character in mythology named Narcissus, a handsome young man who was very proud of his good looks.

The Suffix *-ism*
The noun suffix *-ism* means "the doctrine of." For example:
- If someone is known for his *stoicism*, he is able to suffer without complaint. The word comes from an area in ancient Athens where the philosopher Zeno taught the virtues of emotional control and physical endurance.
- Communities plagued by *vandalism* are subject to the destruction of property by lawless gangs. The Vandals were a warlike German tribe who attacked Rome in the fifth century, destroying much of the city.
- Voters are often accused of *cynicism* in their attitudes toward politicians. They are distrustful of the motives and actions of others. Such cynics take their name from a group in early Greece, the Cynics, who were generally critical of society.

Word List 12: Practice Table

Word	Pronun- ciation	Noun Form	Verb Form	Adjective Form	Adverb Form
narcissistic	nahr-si-SIS-tik	narcissist, narcissism		narcissistic	
cynicism	SIN-i-siz-um	cynic, cynicism		cynical	cynically
pasteurize	PAS-chur-ize	pasteuriza-tion, pasteurizer	pasteurize		
vandalism					
bowdlerize					
utopian					
mesmerize					
academic					
stoicism					
draconian					

The Suffix *-ian*

The adjective ending *-ian* means "having the characteristics of." For example:

- A *utopian* society is an ideal community. This word is based on the book Utopia by Sir Thomas More.
- A *draconian* law is harsh and punitive. The word is derived from the Athenian lawmaker Draco, who was known for his harsh code of laws.

Other Suffixes

Here are some other suffixes you may want to recognize and use. As you consider each suffix, see what other examples you can add.

Noun Endings

Suffix	Meaning	Example	Your Example(s)
-tion	"state of"	situation	_____
-ment	"quality of"	sentiment	_____
-ity	"state of being"	gravity	_____
-ology	"study of"	audiology	_____
-y or *-ry*	"state of"	penury	_____
-ness	"state of"	loneliness	_____

Verb Endings

Suffix	Meaning	Example	Your Example(s)
-ate	"to bring about"	liberate	_____
-ify	"to make"	ratify	_____

Adjective Endings

Suffix	Meaning	Example	Your Example(s)
-ic	"causing"	simplistic	_____
-ive	"in the nature of"	descriptive	_____

-ful	"having much of"	harmful	_____
-less	"without"	harmless	_____

Fill in the Blanks

Write the form of the word needed in each sentence.

1. He was the most self-centered, n_____ person she had ever known. (*Clue:* adjective form.)

2. Someone who is highly educated and interested in intellectual pursuits could be called a(n) a_____. (*Clue:* noun form.)

3. Many long for a u_____ society in which all human problems are solved by thoughtful discussion and negotiation. (*Clue:* adjective form.)

4. If you wanted to p_____ your milk, you would have to heat it to 145° F for a short period of time and then let it cool before drinking it. (*Clue:* verb form.)

5. His s_____ attitude despite his terrible pain made him a hero to his family and the medical staff who cared for him. (*Clue:* adjective form.)

6. Some feel that recent welfare reform is d_____ in its impact on services for children. (*Clue:* adjective form.)

Complete the Words

Fill in the missing letters to spell the words in this lesson.

7. cyn__ __ism

8. mes__ __ __ize

9. a__ __ __ __mic

10. van__ __ __ism

11. bo__ __ __ __rize

Meanings for Word List 12

This box contains the words for this lesson, with their pronunciations and meanings.

narcissistic (narh-si-SIS-tik; adjective): self-absorbed and conceited

cynicism (SIN-i-siz-um; noun): distrust of the motives of others

pasteurize (PAS-chur-ize): to kill bacteria in milk or other liquids by heating it for a short period of time and then letting it cool

vandalism (VAN-dul-iz-um; noun): the destruction of property by lawless bands

bowdlerize (BODE-lur-ize): to shorten or modify (a book, for example) in a conservative manner

utopian (yoo-TOH-pee-un; adjective): describing an ideal society

mesmerize (MEZ-mur-yze; verb): to fascinate; to hold spellbound

academic (ak-uh-DEM-ik): one who is highly educated or associated with an institution of higher learning or views the world in a scholarly way; having to do with higher education

stoicism (STOH-i-siz-um; noun): the ability to bear pain without complaint

PRACTICE EXERCISES

See how well you know the words in this lesson.

Matching Opposites

Match each word in column A with its *opposite* in column B.

	A		B
12.	_____academic	**a.**	trusting
13.	_____narcissistic	**b.**	complicate
14.	_____cynical	**c.**	complaining
15.	_____stoic	**d.**	untaught
16.	_____bowdlerize	**e.**	modest

Unscramble

Unscramble the letters to spell words in this lesson:

17. davalnmis   _____

18. cicnisym   _____

19. ranscistis   _____

20. radnocain   _____

ANSWERS

Here's a clue to one word in this lesson:

A **narcissist** may appear to take his name from a flower that you might recognize: *narcissus*. Actually, the flower in turn gets its name from the mythological Narcissus, a handsome fellow who fell in love with his reflection in the water and then drowned as he tried to kiss it. The flower got its name because it grows facing the water.

Word List 12: Answer Table

Word	Pronun-ciation	Noun Form	Verb Form	Adjective Form	Adverb Form
narcissistic	nahr-si-SIS-tik	narcissist, narcissism		narcissistic	
cynicism	SIN-i-siz-um	cynic, cynicism		cynical	cynically
pasteurize	PAS-chur-ize	pasteuriza-tion, pasteurizer	pasteurize		
vandalism	VAN-dul-iz-um	vandal, vandalism	vandalize		
bowdlerize	BODE-lur-ize	bowdler-izer, bowd-lerization, bowdler-ism	bowdler-ize		

utopian	yoo-TOH-pee-um	utopia		utopian	
mesmerize	MEZ-mur-eyze		mesmerize	mesmer-izing	
academic	ak-uh-DEM-ik	academic		academic	academi-cally
stoicism	STOH-i-siz-um	stoic, stoicism		stoic	stoically
draconian	dray-KOH-nee-un			draconian	

A Closer Look

Suffixes

Here are some examples of noun, verb, and adjective endings that you may have filled in. You may have chosen different words.

Noun Endings

- *-tion:* opposition, assumption
- *-ment:* commitment, assortment
- *-ity:* hostility, dependability
- *-ology:* biology, physiology
- *-y* or *ry:* perjury, typography
- *-ness:* happiness, fondness

Verb Endings

- *-ate:* initiate, animate
- *-ify:* notify, identify

Adjective Endings

- *-ic:* toxic, fantastic
- *-ive:* cooperative, captive
- *-ful:* helpful, colorful
- *less:* sleepless, joyless

Fill in the Blanks

1. narcissistic
2. academic
3. utopian
4. pasteurize
5. stoic
6. draconian

Complete the Words

7. cyn*i*cism
8. mes*mer*ize
9. a*cade*mic
10. van*dali*sm
11. bo*wdle*rize

Practice Exercises

Matching Opposites

12. d
13. e
14. a
15. c
16. b

Unscramble

17. vandalism
18. cynicism
19. narcissist
20. draconian

IN SHORT

In this lesson, you have met additional eponyms based on proper names, and you've seen how word endings can identify the different roles words play according to their use in sentences. As you meet a new word while you read, listen to the radio, watch TV, or have a conversation, remember that its suffix may tell you *how* that word is "working" in the sentence.

13

WORDS FROM OTHER LANDS AND LANGUAGES

In this lesson, you will encounter words that come from other languages. The English language is full of words that have either developed from words from other languages or have been imported directly from those languages into English. Since the sight and sound of many of these words are unfamiliar to many people, this lesson also introduces a new word-meaning strategy: using context.

In the next few pages, you will look at a number of interesting words and consider two specific types of context clues to understanding: context clues **by definition** and context clues **by contrast**.

CONTEXT CLUES BY DEFINITION

When we say context clues "by definition," we mean clues to the meaning of a word given directly in the sentence. Such clues clarify word meaning on the spot. Usually, this is done by simply adding a synonym or phrase in the sentence to "tell" the meaning of the less-familiar word.

He had an extensive *repertoire*, or *collection*, of jokes and stories.

In this sentence, the word *collection*, probably the more familiar word, has been added to help the reader understand the meaning of *repertoire*.

CONTEXT CLUES BY CONTRAST

Context clues by *contrast* are clues written to define a new word by indicating the exact opposite of its meaning.

Although he thought his ideas were very *avant garde*, in many ways, they were quite *old-fashioned*.

In contrast to *old-fashioned*, the phrase *avant garde* means "brand new" or "ahead of its time." At the beginning of the sentence, the word *although* points the reader to the logical contrast between the terms that will follow.

WORD LIST 13

For the words in this lesson, do as before:

- Read all the sentences.
- Underline bold words you already know and can define by sight.
- Put a star over bold words that seem familiar but that you cannot define by sight.
- Circle words in bold that are unfamiliar to you.

Sentences

This first group of sentences contain context clues by definition.

barrio

In interviews, the author often referred to his youth in the **barrio**, the Spanish-speaking neighborhood where he had lived for most of his life.

He considered himself a **connoisseur**, an expert judge, of fine cooking.

They sat in a **bistro**, or restaurant, along the boulevard.

Ever since he was a young boy, he dreamed of becoming an **admiral**, a commander of a ship, in the Navy.

Caught in the **maelstrom**, the whirlwind, of a harassment suit, Bob decided to resign from his position to avoid causing the company any more problems.

For someone just out of college, she had a lot of business **savvy**, or smarts, and, as a result, was hired by a high-profile company.

The wealthy industrialist was sometimes too busy to attend business meetings, so he sent an **ambassador**, an authorized representative, in his place.

The **pundits**, or so-called experts, commented on the progress of the trial.

Here are some sentences that contain context clues by contrast.

Despite his youth in the **ghetto**, he said that he would make a place for himself in the wider world.

Officials claimed that racial integration had been achieved in South Africa, but it seemed clear that many voters still favored policies of **apartheid**.

apartheid

Though the play was hardly a success, it was not nearly the **fiasco** that some critics described.

Though she said she was on a tight budget, Tiffany seemed to give herself **carte blanche** to buy new shoes.

The young man wore an air of worldly sophistication, but in unguarded moments, his basic **naiveté** was obvious.

naiveté

Despite tensions on both sides, the **détente** lessened the strain between the two countries.

Since Harold could not afford a genuine diamond, he presented his fiancée with an **ersatz** stone.

Now fill in the tables on the next page, using the clues provided in the sentences.

Word List 13A: Practice Table

Word	Original Language	Foreign Meaning	Phrase in Sentence That Tells Meaning of the Word
barrio	Spanish	barrier	"the Spanish-speaking neighborhood"
connoisseur	French	one who knows	"an expert judge"
bistro	French	a small restaurant or tavern	
admiral	Arabic	commander of the sea	
maelstrom	Dutch	grinding current	
savvy	Spanish	wise	
ambassador	Celtic	servant, henchman; one who goes about	
pundit	Hindi	a learned man	

Word List 13B: Practice Table

Word	Original Language	Foreign Meaning	Phrase in Sentence That Tells Meaning of the Word
ghetto	Italian	a section of Venice where Jews were required to live	"the wider world"
apartheid	Afrikaans	being apart	
fiasco	Italian	little flask	
carte blanche	French	blank check	
naiveté	French	natural	
détente	French	relaxing of tensions	
ersatz	German	fake; artificial	

A CLOSER LOOK
Syllables

Divide the words into syllables:

1. barrio _____

2. admiral _____

3. fiasco _____

4. ersatz _____

5. bistro _____

6. ghetto _____

Spelling

Practice spelling these words by filling in the missing letters in the words:

7. apart__ __ __d

8. amba__ __ __ __or

9. ma__ __ __ __rom

10. nai__ __té

11. dét__ __te

Meanings for Word List 13

Here are words and definitions for Lesson 13. Pay special attention to their phonetic spellings because many foreign words sound differently than their appearance would suggest

pundit (PUN-dit): an authority on something. This word is most often heard with regard to politics

apartheid (uh-PAHRT-hayt): policy of official separation of the races in South Africa

barrio (BAH-ree-oh): a Spanish-speaking area in a city

bistro (BEE-stroe): a small restaurant or tavern

carte blanche (kahrt BLAHNCH): unlimited authority or permission

admiral (AD-mir-uhl): the commander in charge of a fleet

maelstrom (MAYL-struhm): a violent or turbulent situation

connoisseur (kon-us-SOOR): an authority on the quality of food, wine, art, etc.

détente (day-TAHNT): the relaxing of international tensions

fiasco (fee-AS-koh): a complete failure

ersatz (ER-zatz): fake or synthetic, usually with reference to a material substance or fabric; serving as a substitute, as in *ersatz coffee*

ghetto (GET-toh): a place of separation or isolation for a specific group; traditionally this was an area where Jews were required, by law or custom, to live

naiveté (nah-eev-TAY): simplicity, innocence

savvy (SA-vee): well informed and perceptive

ambassador (am-BAS-uh-der): an authorized messenger or representative

PRACTICE EXERCISES

How well do you know the words in this lesson? Answer the questions and find out.

Unscrambling

Unscramble these letters to make the words from this lesson.

12. saobrmaads   _____

13. rabrio   _____

14. tribos   _____

15. teghto   _____

16. ofcias   _____

17. rdlaaim   _____

Yes or No?

Answer the questions with Yes or No, according to the meaning of the italicized word.

18. _____ Would a *pundit* be well informed about foreign policy?

19. _____ Would you give *carte blanche* to a spendthrift spouse?

20. _____ Would you want a *connoisseur* to make a wine choice for you?

21. _____ Would you expect *naiveté* from a hardened criminal?

22. _____ Would you expect to find a separation of the races under a regime that sanctioned *apartheid*?

ANSWERS

Here are three examples of how you can use some of the clues you've learned to discover the meaning of words in this lesson:

Barrio looks like *barrier.*

Apartheid has within it the word *apart.*

Naiveté sounds like *naïve.*

Word List 13A: Answer Table

Word	Original Language	Foreign Meaning	Phrase in Sentence That Tells Meaning of the Word
barrio	Spanish	barrier	"the Spanish-speaking neighborhood"
connoisseur	French	one who knows	"an expert judge"
bistro	French	a small restaurant or tavern	"restaurant"
admiral	Arabic	commander of the sea	"a commander of a ship"
maelstrom	Dutch	grinding current	"the whirlwind"
savvy	Spanish	wise	"smarts"
ambassador	Celtic	servant, henchman; one who goes about	"an authorized representative"
pundit	Hindi	a learned man	"so-called experts"

Word List 13B: Answer Table

Word	Original Language	Foreign Meaning	Phrase in Sentence That Tells Meaning of the Word
ghetto	Italian	a section of Venice where Jews were required to live	"the wider world"
apartheid	Afrikaans	being apart	"racial integration"
fiasco	Italian	little flask	"success"
carte blanche	French	blank check	"tight budget"
naiveté	French	natural	"worldly sophistication"
détente	French	relaxing of tensions	"tensions"
ersatz	German	fake; artificial	"genuine"

A Closer Look

Syllables

1. bar-ri-o
2. ad-mir-al
3. fi-as-co
4. er-satz
5. bis-tro
6. ghet-to

Spelling

7. apart*hei*d
8. amba*ssad*or
9. ma*elst*rom
10. nai*vet*é
11. dé*ten*te

Practice Exercises

Unscrambling

12. ambassador
13. barrio
14. bistro
15. ghetto
16. fiasco
17. admiral

Yes or No?

18. Yes
19. No
20. Yes
21. No
22. Yes

IN SHORT

In this lesson, you've looked at words from other languages and cultures that might be unfamiliar to you and difficult to read from sight, sound, or structure. You have seen how two types of context clues—definition and contrast—help determine word meaning.

LESSON

14

WORD MEANING FROM CONTEXT

In this lesson, you'll discover more foreign words that have made their way into common English usage. You'll learn two new types of context clues that can help you understand what these new words mean and how they're used.

In this lesson, you will continue to encounter words from other languages that may not look or sound familiar, and so you will have to draw their meaning from the context of the sentence. You will learn two more kinds of context clues that will help you grasp the meaning of the words you see or hear. They are context clues **by example** and context clues **by restatement**.

CONTEXT CLUES BY EXAMPLE AND BY RESTATEMENT

In context clues *by example*, the writer gives you an illustration of an unfamiliar word.

> His vast knowledge of art and good food singled him out as a true *connoisseur*.

In this sentence, the example of his "vast knowledge" expresses the meaning of *connoisseur*.

In context clues by *restatement*, the writer adds a sentence to add information that will help a reader determine word meaning.

> Evelyn's birthday party was a *fiasco*. It was such a disaster that we decided to throw her another party next month.

In this instance, the second sentence defines the highlighted word *fiasco* from the first sentence as a "disaster."

WORD LIST 14

As you work with this lesson's words:

- Read all the sentences.
- Underline bold words you already know and can define by sight.
- Put a star over bold words that seem familiar but that you cannot define by sight.
- Circle words in bold that are unfamiliar to you.

Sentences

In this first group of sentences, you will find example clues for the bold words:

Introducing her boss's girlfriend as his wife was a **faux pas** that caused the new secretary great embarrassment.

When the rebels quickly took control of the country, the **coup d'état** became a reality.

Despite his fear, he stood up to the rioters in a show of **bravado**.

bravado

The security cameras in the jewelry store were a silent **caveat** to would-be thieves.

The movie star's group of friends and associates made a **coterie** that followed her everywhere.

Now notice the restatement clues for the highlighted words in the following sentences:

The celebrity preferred to travel **incognito**. He disguised his appearance so that he would be unrecognizable to the public.

incognito

The **bouquet** of 12 roses was tied together by a white ribbon. The grouping of flowers perfectly complemented the bride's dress.

Although the **graffiti** painted on the wall was considered a defamation of public property, it was a beautiful work of art displayed in a public place.

The **mannequins** in the store window were clothed in the new fall collection. The life-sized representations of the human body were the perfect way to show off the styles.

The teacher established an excellent **rapport** with the students. Her close relationship with them helped her understand their needs.

Now look again at the words in the sentences you just read, and fill in the missing information in the practice tables on the next page. Notice again how the foreign words sound in English.

Word List 14A: Practice Table

Word	Pronunciation	Foreign Meaning	Example Clue from Sentence
faux pas	foh PAH	a "false step" (French)	"introducing his boss's girlfriend to his wife"
coup d'état	koo day-TAH	a "stroke of state" (French)	"when the rebels . . . took control of the country
bravado	bruh-VAH-doh	"false courage" (Spanish)	
caveat	KAHV-ee-at	a "warning" (Latin)	
coterie	KOHT-uh-ree	a "group or clique" (French	

Word List 14B: Practice Table

Word	Pronunciation	Foreign Meaning	Example Clue from Sentence
incognito	in-kog-NEE-toh	"unknown" (Italian)	"disguised his appearance"
bouquet	boo-KAYE	"thicket" (French)	
graffiti	gruh-FEE-tee	"a scratch" (Italian)	
mannequin	MAN-uh-kin	"little man" (Dutch)	
rapport	rap-POHR	"close relation-ship" (French)	

A CLOSER LOOK
Consonants

1. Four words from this lesson that have the hard sound of *c* are

_____, _____,

_____, and _____.

2. The above words have the hard *c* sound because

_____.

3. The *g* in the word *graffiti* has the _____ sound because

_____.

4. There is a silent letter at the end of these three French words:

_____ , _____, and

_____.

Syllables

Divide these words into syllables.

5. graffiti   _____

6. bravado   _____

7. mannequin   _____

8. rapport   _____

Punctuation Clues to Context

Punctuation, particularly commas, can often point you to context clues to word meaning. Note in the three examples that follow how such clues are set off from the rest of the sentence by commas:

- **Contrasts** are often introduced by commas:

   A proposal currently before the legislature would permit welfare recipients to receive vouchers for needed supplies, *rather than checks for cash.*

- **Definitions** are often set off by commas:

   Many in Congress fear that increased farm subsidies, *or price supports,* will lead to tax hikes that could alienate their constituents in an election year.

- **Examples** can be set off with a semicolon and a comma:

   There is hope that a bipartisan coalition in Congress can expedite flood relief to the Midwest; that is, that they will pass emergency legislation that will *speed up* aid to the stricken area.

Meanings for Word List 14

The box contains this lesson's words, with their pronunciations and meanings.

faux pas (foh PAH): a social error

coup d'état (koo day-TAH): a sudden overthrow of government

bravado (brah-VAH-doh): pretended courage

caveat (KAV-ee-aht): a warning meaning "at your own risk"

coterie (KOHT-uh-ree): a close group of friends or supporters; an entourage

incognito (in-kog-NEE-toh): in disguise

bouquet (boo-KAYE): a small cluster or arrangement of flowers

graffiti (gruh-FEE-tee): a drawing or inscription made on a wall or other surface visible to the public

mannequin (MAN-uh-kin): a life-size full or partial representation of the human body used to display clothes

rapport (ra-POHR): close communication between people

PRACTICE EXERCISES

See how well you know the words in Word List 14.

What Type of Clue?

Read the following sentences. Tell whether each sentence has context clues by definition (**D**), by contrast (**C**), by example (**E**), or by restatement (**R**).

9. _____ He displayed a kind of *bravado*, or false courage, that disguised his real fear.

10. _____ She believed she was traveling *incognito*, but her famous face was not hidden by her disguise.

11. _____ The counselor's most difficult job was to establish a good *rapport* with the clients. It was vital that she have close communication with the families with whom she would work.

12. _____ The bride carried a *bouquet* of flowers made up of a bunch of roses.

13. _____ It was clear that the *graffiti* on the wall was painted by a talented artist, but it still had to be removed.

14. _____ Drinking from the finger bowl at the fancy dinner party was a *faux pas* that humiliated the young girl from the country.

15. _____ The Surgeon General issued a strongly worded *caveat* about the dangers of tobacco, but many ignored the warning and continued to smoke.

True or False?

Mark the following sentences as True or False, according to the meaning of the highlighted word:

16. _____A *coup d'état* is an intimate conversation.

17. _____After a wedding, the bride usually throws her *bouquet* into the crowd of guests.

18. _____You are likely to have a good *rapport* with people you have known for a long time.

19. _____If you commit a *faux pas*, you will probably be embarrassed.

20. _____A *caveat* is an expensive gourmet treat.

ANSWERS

Here are some clues to the meanings of words in this lesson:

Bravado looks like *brave*.

Incognito has a structure clue in it (*-cogn-*), which looks like *recognize*.

Word List 14A: Answer Table

Word	Pronunciation	Foreign Meaning	Example Clue from Sentence
faux pas	foh PAH	a "false step" (French)	"introducing his boss's girlfriend to his wife"
coup d'état	koo day-TAH	a "stroke of state" (French)	"when the rebels . . . took control of the country
bravado	bruh-VAH-doh	"false courage" (Spanish)	"he stood up to the riders"
caveat	KAHV-ee-at	a "warning" (Latin)	"security cameras"
coterie	KOHT-uh-ree	a "group or clique" (French	"group of friends and associates"

Word List 14B: Answer Table

Word	Pronunciation	Foreign Meaning	Example Clue from Sentence
incognito	in-kog-NEE-toh	"unknown" (Italian)	"disguised his appearance"
bouquet	boo-KAYE	"thicket" (French)	"grouping of flowers"
graffiti	gruh-FEE-tee	"a scratch" (Italian)	"a beautiful work of art displayed in a public place
mannequin	MAN-uh-kin	"little man" (Dutch)	"the life-sized representations of the human body"
rapport	rap-POHR	"close relationship" (French)	"close relationship"

A Closer Look

Consonants

1. coup d'état, caveat, coterie, and incognito

2. each *c* is not followed by *e*, *i*, or *y*

3. soft; it's not followed by *e*, *i*, or a *y*.

4. rapport, faux pas, bouquet

Syllables

5. graf-fi-ti

6. bra-va-do

7. mann-e-quin

8. rap-port

Practice Exercises

What Type of Clue?

9. d

10. c

11. r

12. r

13. e

14. e

15. d

True or False?

16. False

17. True

18. True

19. True

20. False

IN SHORT

In this lesson, you had an opportunity to notice some specific ways that writers can signal the meaning of a word, either by means of an example or by restating the word's meaning in another sentence or phrase. Not all context clues found in ordinary writing are necessarily this specific, but being aware of the kinds of context clues writers use can be helpful in figuring out the meanings of new words that come your way. You have now learned all the word meaning strategies you'll need to figure out what words mean. The rest of the lessons in this book will help you learn new words using these strategies.

WORDS FROM COMPUTER TECHNOLOGY

In this lesson, you will plunge into the mysteries of computer jargon. *Jargon* is a word that means the "specialized language of a particular job or field of interest," and the field of computers has plenty of it.

Computers are all around us; we encounter them in schools, in the workplace, and at home. In any of these locations, or even on the bus, on a street corner, or at a party, you might hear:

> "So I booted up and found I had a glitch in my file server that crashed my CPU."

> "I wanted a 95-gigabyte hard drive, but I couldn't get it unless I could get more RAM."

As these excerpts of dialogue suggest, unless you work in the computer field or use a computer regularly, much of its terminology may sound like a foreign language.

Get ready to change all that! You're about to be brought up to date by learning words for several of the most commonly used computer features, activities, and equipment.

WORD LIST 15

For the words in this lesson, do as before:

- Read all the sentences.
- Underline bold words you already know and can define by sight.
- Put a star over bold words that seem familiar but that you cannot define by sight.
- Circle words in bold that are unfamiliar to you.

Sentences

In the following sentences, see if you can figure out what the words or terms mean from the context clues in the sentences.

upload

I am going to remotely **upload** my files at work to my computer at home. This way, I can just copy the information directly, saving time.

He used a **compact disc** to transfer information from his office computer to his home computer. There was just enough room left to store all of the pertinent files.

The Internet **browser** she uses now accesses websites much faster than the old one she was using.

Internet

High-speed devices called **modems** allow computers to speak with one another **online** through telephone lines in a network of computers we call the **Internet**.

She said, "Leave a message on my **voicemail**. My **e-mail** is already full." These two kinds of electronic messaging features are replacing "snail mail," or traditional letters sent through the postal service.

The **hacker** used the pointing tool known as a **mouse** to **access**, or enter, computer networks and systems illegally.

On the video screen, or **monitor**, a number of **icons** will be visible. These small pictures identify an application or program on a computer.

Websites are locations on the World Wide Web, an international network of computer connections that allows people to communicate with each other around the world.

She entered the numbers on the **spreadsheet** program, which organized her data into columns and rows on the screen.

Now, based on these sentences, fill in the information in the table on the next page.

A CLOSER LOOK
Acronyms

In addition to the words and terms used in the sentences you just read, the field of computer and communication technology is loaded with *acronyms*, or words that are made up of the first letters of a group of words or a phrase. For example:

- HTML stands for "**h**yper**t**ext **m**arkup **l**anguage."
- JPEG stands for **J**oint **P**hotographic **E**xperts **G**roup and is a computer file format for the compression and storage of usually high-quality photographic digital images.

Note that acronyms differ from abbreviations in that you pronounce them as words, not individual letters (JPEG is pronounced "J-PEG," not "jay-pee-ee-gee").

Some additional acronyms related to the computer field are:

RAM: "**r**andom-**a**ccess **m**emory," or memory that can be used to store and run programs. Any information in RAM is lost when the power is turned off unless that information has been stored in another storage system, such as a disk, beforehand.

ROM: "**r**ead-**o**nly **m**emory," or memory that allows access to information stored on a hard drive or compact disc

DOS: **d**isk-**o**perating **s**ystem

CD-ROM: a **c**ompact **d**isc (abbreviated "CD") on which a large amount of information can be stored. [*Note:* CD-ROM combines an abbreviation (CD) with an acronym (ROM).]

WYSIWYG (pronounced "WI-zee-wig"): stands for "what you see is what you get." In the computer field, this term means that a hard copy, or printed page, of your text or graphic will look just as the information appears on the computer monitor.

Word List 15: Practice Table

Word	Pronunciation	Part of Speech	Context Clue
upload	UP-lohd	verb	restatement
compact disc	COM-pakt disk	noun	example
browser	BROW-zer	noun	definition
modem			
online			
Internet			
voicemail			
email			
hacker			
mouse			
access			
monitor			
icon			
website			
spreadsheet			

Compound Words

Remember that *compound words* are made up of two separate words that combine to form one new word. Find three words in Word List 15 that are compounds.

1. _____, _____, and

_____.

Homographs

You learned about homographs in Lesson 2; they're words that have the same sound and the same spelling but have one or more different meanings. In this lesson, there are four homographs. In the following exercise, one meaning for each word is given to you. What other meanings do you know?

2. *mouse:* a pointing device on a computer; *or*

_____

_____

_____

3. *icon:* a small image that denotes a particular word or function on a computer; *or* _____

_____

_____

4. *disc:* a small, magnetic circle that stores computer information; *or*

_____

_____

_____

5. *monitor:* the part of the computer that holds the video screen; *or*

_____

_____

_____

Syllables

Divide each of the following words into syllables.

6. modem   _____

7. browser   _____

8. monitor   _____

9. access   _____

10. hacker   _____

Meanings for Word List 15

Now take a look at the pronunciations and definitions of the words in this lesson. See how close you came to getting them right.

upload (UP-lohd): to transfer files from a main computer to another one in a remote location

compact disc (COM-pakt disk): a small optical disk in which data is encoded digitally

browser (BROW-zer): the program that serves as your access to the Internet

modem (MOH-duhm): a device that allows computers to interact with each other through the Internet by means of telephone wires

online (ON-LYNE): having access to the Internet by means of a modem

Internet (IN-tuhr-net): the network of computer connections that allow people to communicate with others through their computers

voicemail (VOYS mayl): a system or device that answers the telephone and records messages

e-mail (EE-mayl): an electronic message system that stores and retrieves correspondence through the computer

hacker (HAK-uhr): a person who invades the computer systems of other people, often illegally

mouse (MOWSE): a small plastic device connected by a cord to the computer. It is used as a pointing tool to access computer functions

access (AK-ses): the action by which programs and files are opened for use on the computer

monitor (MON-i-tuhr): the part of the computer that holds the video screen

icon (EYE-kon): a small picture or symbol that identifies a specific program or operation on a computer

website (WEB syte): a location on the World Wide Web, an international network of computers. At these locations, users can do research, promote services and products, share ideas, respond to world events, and socialize with each other

spreadsheet (SPRED-sheet): a computer program that organizes numerical data into rows and columns

PRACTICE EXERCISES
See how well you know the words in this lesson.

Choose the Correct Word
Circle the correct form of each word below.

11. You need to go (inline / online / underline) to use the Internet.

12. To begin a computer function, you must (excess / accept / access) the program on the computer.

13. To leave a message on the computer, you should use (e-mail / voicemail / snail mail).

14. You must beware of the (backer / heckler / hacker) who could use your computer system illegally.

15. The video screen on your computer is the (monitor / monogram / monolith).

Yes or No?
Answer the following questions with Yes or No, depending on the meaning of the italicized words.

16. _____ *Charlotte's Website* is a famous children's book.

17. _____ You would call a computer *hacker* to repair your modem.

18. _____ The Internet *browser* you use serves as your main access point to the Internet.

19. _____ A *compact disc* digitally encodes information.

20. _____ A *spreadsheet* is necessary for camping trips.

ANSWERS

Here are two clues for two of this lesson's words:

Upload is a compound word, both parts of which should look familiar.

Internet has the prefix *inter-*, which means "between or among." The Internet shares information among millions of computers.

Check the table you filled in against the one that follows.

Word List 15: Answer Table

Word	Pronunciation	Part of Speech	Context Clue
upload	UP-lohd	verb	restatement
compact disc	COM-pakt disk	noun	example
browser	BROW-zer	noun	definition
modem	MOH-duhm	noun	definition
online	ON-LYNE	adverb (tells how); or adjective (tells what type of)	example
Internet	IN-tuhr-net	noun	definition
voicemail	VOYS-mayl	noun	contrast
email	EE mayl	noun	contrast
hacker	HAK-uhr	noun	example
mouse	MOWSE	noun	definition

access	AK-ses	verb	definition
monitor	MON-i-tuhr	noun	definition
icon	EYE-kon	noun	restatement
website	WEB-syte	noun	definition
spreadsheet	SPRED-sheet	noun	definition

A Closer Look

Compound Words

1. upload, voicemail, spreadsheet

Homographs

2. a small rodent

3. a religious picture such as those seen in the Eastern Orthodox faith, or a symbol of a particular sphere of life. For example, we say that certain celebrities are *fashion icons*. We admire them as people who set current clothing style.

4. any flat circular object

5. as a noun, "someone who supervises," for example, a particular group of children or the activity of something. As a verb, *monitor* means "to watch something closely."

Syllables

6. mo-dem

7. brow-ser

8. mon-it-or

9. ac-cess

10. hack-er

Practice Exercises

Choose the Correct Word	Yes or No?
11. online	**16.** No
12. access	**17.** No
13. e-mail	**18.** Yes
14. hacker	**19.** Yes
15. monitor	**20.** No

IN SHORT

The computer industry is a rapidly changing field; new words spring up often. In this lesson, you were introduced to words associated with computers, including some homographs and acronyms.

LESSON

16

IDIOMS AND VOCABULARY VARIATIONS

In this lesson, you will meet a number of expressions that sound familiar but are hard to define outside of the context in which they are used. They're called *idioms*. Although they don't always follow the general rules of word usage, they are an integral part of any language and are important for you to know.

An *idiom* can sometimes mean one of a number of things, depending on how it's used within a sentence. In its simplest form, an idiom is an everyday term or expression whose meaning evolved over time as it was used in conversation and informal writing. You will get a better idea of what idioms are by looking at these examples:

- I was *tied up* at the office until late last night.
- He was *on the phone* when I got to his house.
- The candidate's *spin doctors* were on hand to offer comment on the campaign.

Taken literally, these sentences bring to mind peculiar pictures of people roped to their office chairs, perched on top of telephones, or whirling through hospitals! When you look at them in context, however, you know that the first means that someone was delayed at work, the second, that a man was talking on the phone, and the third, that there were people able to interpret a political office seeker's actions in a favorable light. All of these expressions are idioms, and you will see other such idioms in the next few pages.

WORD LIST 16

As you read the following sentences, note the common idioms.

- Read all the sentences.
- Underline bold words you already know and can define by sight.
- Put a star over bold words that seem familiar but that you cannot define by sight.
- Circle words in bold that are unfamiliar to you.

Sentences

She had never played the piano in public, but when offered a chance to play professionally, she decided to **give it a shot**.

You have to **watch out** for hidden costs in appliance contracts.

He decided to **take a stab** at making his own garden mulch this year.

He tended to **laugh off** her attempts to talk seriously to him.

She pleaded with him to **hold off** on his decision until she could make another offer.

Because she was a nationally ranked tennis player at the young age of eight, she suffered from **burnout** and gave up the game by the age of 12.

I didn't want to tell him the bad news in public because I knew he would **fly off the handle**.

Because she is known as the **life of the party**, she is invited to all social gatherings.

He was angry about having to **cool his heels** in the waiting room for over an hour.

By the time they balanced the increased labor costs with the higher consumer demand, they declared the result to **be a wash**.

He is the **spitting image** of his father, but his brother looked more like their mother.

She was afraid that after all these years, she might not be **up to the job** of raising young children.

By and large he liked his new job.

The gangster went out the back door and managed to **give the slip** to the agents who were trying to question him.

Once in a blue moon, they would order Chinese food for a special treat.

In the table on the next page, translate the idioms into your own words.

A CLOSER LOOK
How Idioms Work

The word *idiom* is derived from the Latin *idio*, referring to the self. An *idiosyncrasy*, for example, is a habit or custom peculiar to one's self. An idiom is seen as any kind of language use that has gained wide usage in that particular language. An idiom is peculiar not to an individual person but to an individual culture's use of language.

Here are some other things to keep in mind about idioms:

- Idioms can be confused with *clichés*, *colloquialisms*, and *slang*.
  - *Clichés* (klee-SHAYZ) are overused phrases that have remained in the language for a long time. "Pretty as a picture," "right as rain," and "selling like hotcakes" are examples of clichés. They are *too* well known to English speakers. Through overuse, their impact is lessened.

    cliché

  - *Colloquialisms* (koh-LOH-kwee-uhl-iz-ums) are expressions that may be appropriate in informal speech but are incorrect in formal writing. The use of "should of" for "should have" and "plan on going" instead of "planning to go" are examples of colloquialisms.

Word List 16: Practice Table

Idiom	Translation
give it a shot	try
watch out	be alert to
take a stab at	
laugh off	
hold off	
burnout	
fly off the handle	
life of the party	
cool his heels	
be a wash	
spitting image	
up to the job	
by and large	
give the slip to	
once in a blue moon	

- *Slang* is informal usage that is often peculiar to a particular age or occupational group. Examples of slang are "tellin' it like it is" or "What's going down?"

- Idiomatic phrases in English include hundreds of verbs paired with smaller words (prepositions) that change the meaning of the verb. *Watching out for* (being alert to) something is different from *watching over* (attending to) something. You might *get up* early one morning so you can *get away* on a vacation to France, where you hope to *get by* with your high-school French so you can *get along* with the natives.

- All languages have their own idioms, which can make translation from one language to another a bit difficult. Even different cultures that speak the same language can have trouble understanding each other's idioms. For instance, people in the United Kingdom use idioms that are different from those used in the United States.

If an Englishman has "knocked up" his girlfriend, he simply has knocked on her door. In American English, the slang expression *knocked up* means something very different—he would have gotten her pregnant!

What we in the United States call an "apartment building," the British call a "block of flats."

In Britain, expensive real estate is "upmarket." Similar property in America is "upscale."

Slang, Colloquialism, or Cliché?

Tell whether each of the following expressions represents slang, a colloquialism, or a cliché:

1. "She *may of* gone to the movies" is an example of

_____.

2. "The car battery was *dead as a doornail*" is an example of

_____.

3. "*Hang a right* at the next corner" is an example of

_____.

Translate the Idiom

Each of the following idioms is commonly used in England. What do you think each of them means?

4. "Please *ring me up* and tell me all the news." To *ring up* means

_____.

5. "She lived in a *bed-sit* in a shabby area of the city." A *bed-sit* is a

_____.

6. "Don't get your *knickers in a twist* over minor problems!" The phrase *knickers in a twist* means

_____.

HOW IDIOMS ENTER THE LANGUAGE

Some idioms are derived from images rooted in experience; it makes sense that *cool heels* would refer to excessive waiting because, presumably, hot heels result from running hard. You can see that *laughing off* something would have to do with not taking it very seriously.

Then there are idioms that have evolved over long periods of time and have no particular logic or origin: for example, *up to the job*. Somewhere in between are idioms whose meanings made sense once upon a time but now are lost. *Spitting image* has nothing to do with saliva. It's a corruption of "spit and image," and *spit* simply meant "exact likeness." If you know that, the idiom makes sense—but most people don't!

Complete the Idioms

Can you think of idioms that would fit in these sentences?

7. If you are frustrated with your progress, *take a* _____ and come back later.

8. He had been at the job for a long time, and it was time to *put him out to*

_____.

9. She did her job competently, but her _____ *wasn't in it.*

Meanings for Word List 16

Here are the idioms in this lesson, with their translations. How many did you get right?

give it a shot: try for the first time

watch out: be careful

take a stab at: attempt

laugh off: ignore with good humor

hold off: delay

burnout: a point of physical or emotional exhaustion

fly off the handle: to get angry

life of the party: a person who makes things enjoyable for a group of people

cool his heels: wait a long time

be a wash: even out

spitting image: exact likeness

up to the job: capable of doing the job

by and large: as a general rule

give the slip to: escape

once in a blue moon: very seldom

PRACTICE EXERCISES

Now, test your idiom know-how.

Fill in the Blanks

Add the idiom needed in each of the following sentences:

10. The stranger in the subway was the _____ of my long-lost cousin.

11. She told her boyfriend he could _____ and wait until she finished getting ready.

12. Though her feelings were hurt by his remark, she was ready to _____ her anger with good humor.

13. Sometimes, when you want to break out of your daily routine, you may have to _____ at something new and exciting.

14. I was worried that she might _____ when I told her she was getting demoted, so I asked my boss to do it instead.

Yes or No?

Answer Yes or No to the following sentences, on the basis of your knowledge of the idioms.

15. _____ If you *burn out* at something, it means that you need the services of an electrician.

16. _____ If it happens *once in a blue moon,* it happens rarely.

17. _____ If you *give the slip* to someone, you hand over your underwear.

18. _____ You have to stand near a window if you are going to *watch out* for something.

19. _____ If you *give something a shot,* you are willing to try.

ANSWERS

cliché: an overused word or phrase that has lost its impact in the language. It is a French word used in English.

How many idioms did you get right? Check your table against the table that follows.

Word List 16: Answer Table

Idiom	Translation
give it a shot	try
watch out	be alert to
take a stab at	try it for the first time
laugh off	take it lightly, ignore it in good humor
hold off	delay
burnout	physical or emotional exhaustion
fly off the handle	to get angry
life of the party	someone who makes things fun

cool his heels	wait a long time
be a wash	even out eventually
spitting image	exactly like in appearance
up to the job	capable of doing something
by and large	generally
give the slip to	escape from
once in a blue moon	very seldom

A Closer Look

Slang, Colloquialism, or Cliché?

1. colloquialism

2. cliché

3. slang

Translate the Idiom

4. to telephone

5. studio apartment

6. to be nervous

Complete the Idiom

7. *break* or *breather*

8. *pasture*

9. *heart*

Practice Exercises

Fill in the Blanks	**Yes or No?**
10. spitting image	**15.** No
11. cool his heels	**16.** Yes
12. laugh off	**17.** No
13. take a shot	**18.** No
14. fly off the handle	**19.** Yes

IN SHORT

In this lesson, you read about *idioms*—expressions peculiar to a particular language that don't usually fit the rules of proper word usage. These idioms may not even be in your dictionary, but they are commonly used and understood nonetheless. You also learned how idioms are different from slang, colloquialisms, and clichés.

NEW AND EMERGING VOCABULARY

In this lesson, you will encounter a number of words and terms that have recently entered American English. These words, called *neologisms* (with the structural clue *neo*, a root that signifies newness!), are created as culture, industry, and technology change. It's important to recognize such new words, and it's fun to watch them come into play in the language we read and speak every day.

Like crabgrass—or wildflowers!—in the spring, new words seem to spring up out of nowhere. One minute, you've never heard of a particular word or expression before, and the next, you seem to see and hear it everywhere. All words, of course, have some point of origin. Words that gain sudden popularity in the language often do so because they've grown out of a common new experience or observation.

Some of the ways that we make new words are by:

- *shortening* longer words—for example, from *gymnasium* to *gym.*
- making up *acronyms* (which you read about in Lesson 15)—such as *snafu*, which means "an error" and derives from the phrase "*s*ituation *n*ormal, *a*ll *f*ouled *u*p."

- blending two words together—as in *camcorder* from **camera** and **recorder**
- adapting people's names to ideas that are associated with them—for example, *Reaganomics*, from **Reagan** and **economics**.

WORD LIST 17

What follows are some words that have recently become part of American English. See how many you recognize.

- Read all the sentences.
- Underline bold words you already know and can define by sight.
- Put a star over bold words that seem familiar but that you cannot define by sight.
- Circle words in bold that are unfamiliar to you.

Sentences

The actress taped a series of **infomercials** for her favorite cosmetic line.

He ended all of his e-mails with an **emoticon** that showed how he was feeling.

To **carjack** someone is no different than to rob a convenience store.

glitterati

A large number of the city's **glitterati** appeared at the performance.

My favorite pants that I own are a pair of brown **cords**.

micromanage

Continuous messages by **fax** made it possible for the CEO to **micromanage** his business even when he was away from the office.

The **emcee** on the telethon was an actor who had also won an award for his **docudrama** on AIDS.

More and more employees are becoming **telecommuters**, who work at home and interact with other employees and managers by computer.

flextime

One of the **perks** of the new position was the **flextime** allowed to employees.

The architect hired a PR firm to do a **multimedia** production tracing the efforts of city planners that led to major **gentrification** projects in poor neighborhoods all over town.

multimedia

Now fill in the table on the next page, according to your understanding of the boldfaced words in the sentences you just read.

A CLOSER LOOK
Shortenings

Sometimes, new words are formed when existing words are shortened; perhaps the shortened form, which often means the same as the longer word, evolves because it is easier to use. The word *fax* is a shortening and respelling of the word *facsimile*; similarly, the word *perk* comes from *perquisite*, which means a benefit of employment.

Fill in some other shortened words.

1. We shorten *fanatic* to _____.

2. We shorten *condominium* to _____.

3. We shorten *influenza* to _____.

4. We shorten *dormitory* to _____.

5. We shorten *delicatessen* to _____.

Acronyms

You learned about acronyms in Lesson 15, when you read that there are a number of words in English that are made up of the first letters of each word of a phrase. The word *emcee* is an odd acronym. It stands for the initials of "Master of Ceremonies" and is used either as a noun (He was the *emcee* of the show) or as a verb (He will *emcee* the show next week).

Can you supply the acronyms?

6. The acronym that refers to the newest employees being the most likely to be laid off first if the company experiences a downturn is

_____.

7. United Nations International Children's Emergency Fund:

_____.

8. What you see is what you get (on a computer):

_____.

9. Congress on Racial Equality: _____.

10. North Atlantic Treaty Organization: _____.

11. Mothers Against Drunk Driving: _____.

12. Young urban professionals: _____.

Word List 17: Practice Table

Words	Possible Sources
infomercial	a blend of *information* and *commerical*
emoticon	a combination of *emotion* and *icon*
LIFO	acronym for "*l*ast *in*, *f*irst *out*"
carjack	
glitterati	
cords	
fax	
micromanage	
emcee	
docudrama	
telecommuter	
perk	
flextime	
multimedia	
gentrification	

Blends

Blends—formed by combining two or more words, or parts of them, into one new word—date back to the eighteenth century in the English language, when Eldridge Gerry, a candidate for office in Massachusetts, redrew the geographical boundary lines to redistribute the election districts so that he would have a better chance of winning. Someone remarked that the resulting district looked like a salamander, and some anonymous wit replied, "No, that's a Gerry-mander!" So that kind of manipulation of voting districts came to be known as *gerrymandering*.

Today's vocabulary is constantly being fueled by new blends. Most of them can be recognized by their structure—that is, by the descriptive nature of the two or more words being blended.

See if you can identify the blends created from the following:

13. A combined dance and exercise program is called

_____.

14. A "sailor" in space is an _____.

15. A comedy based on an ongoing situation is called a   _____.

16. A movie theater that shows many films at once is a _____.

17. A lengthy television production aimed at raising money for a charitable or nonprofit organization is a   _____.

Words from Proper Names

As you saw in Lesson 11, a large number of English words have their source in proper names. Such words, you will recall, are called *eponyms.* Recent vocabulary additions have drawn on people's names, such as the verb *mirandize.* This word is derived from the Miranda decision by the Supreme Court, which requires that police officers warn suspected wrongdoers of their rights to the services of an attorney and protection against self-incrimination. (Notice that words derived from proper names often lose their capital letters.)

A recent addition to conversation is the expression "He's really a Luddite." This means that the person can't cope with the wonders of modern technology. The Luddites were people in the nineteenth century who smashed machinery in opposition to the march of industrialization. As you might expect, they were named after a man named Ned Ludd.

In addition to words based on people's names, vocabulary often evolves from the speakers' associations with brand names of products. Although it is commonly done in everyday conversation, using a proper name to describe all such items, not just those with that particular brand-name, is often inappropriate in published writing. If the brand name item is still under trademark protection, then the writer may actually be infringing upon the trademark rights of the company that owns that brand-name. Nevertheless, people often use these names in conversation.

Fill in the names that describe not only the specific product, but also the whole category of products.

18. Cellophane tape of any kind is usually called _____ tape.

19. Gelatin desserts of any brand are usually called _____.

20. Individual small bandages are called _____.

21. Photocopies are usually run off on the _____, regardless of the name of the copier being used.

22. An insulated container is a _____ bottle.

Meanings for Word List 17

Here are the words from Lesson 17, with their pronunciations and meanings. Did you figure them all out from the sentences?

emoticon (i-MOE-ti-kon): a symbol used in e-mail to indicate emotion or attitude

infomercial (IN-foh-mer-shul): a commercial that is disguised as an information-giving program

LIFO (LYE-foh): a policy that says that the last people to be hired will be the first to be fired (last in, first out)

carjack (KAR-jak): to commit theft of a vehicle, usually while its users are still in it

glitterati (glit-uh-RAH-tee): a combination of *glitter* and *literati*; a trendy word for fashionable and often wealthy people, who, when the term was first used, came from the publishing world but now need not. The *glitterati* are those who are particularly social and visible to the public

cords (KORDZ): trousers made of corduroy, a cotton fabric with vertical ribs

fax (FAKS): a copy of a printed document dispatched by telephone lines by means of a modem; or to dispatch such a document

micromanage (MYE-kroh-man-edj): to closely supervise the management of the daily operations of workers in the company

emcee (em-CEE): the master of ceremonies or host of a performance or program; or to host a performance

docudrama (DOK-yoo-drah-mah): a documentary film that is presented in a dramatic, sometimes fictionalized, format

telecommuter (TEL-uh-kom-yoo-ter): someone who works at home and communicates with the office by computer

perk (PERK): a shortening of *perquisite*, which means a benefit of employment

flextime (FLEKS-tyme): a system of flexible work hours that permits employees to work on a schedule best suited to each individual

multimedia (MUHL-tye-MEE-dee-ah): a format for presentation that includes a variety of media—radio, television, and live performance

gentrification (jen-tri-fi-KAY-shun): the renovating of older, often marginal, neighborhoods for sale to wealthier owners

PRACTICE EXERCISES

Test your mastery of the words in this lesson by doing the following exercises.

Fill in the Blanks

Write in the needed words.

23. Someone who wants to supervise every detail of her employees' performance is someone who wants to _____ the workplace.

24. I don't use _____ in my e-mails because I want to express my sentiment well with words alone.

25. The television miniseries on the American Revolution was a _____ that presented history in a dramatic and artistic way.

26. More and more employees are choosing to become _____ because it lets them work at home and be connected to the office by computer.

27. Working parents benefit from _____,which allows them to plan their working hours in ways that are convenient and productive.

True or False?

Mark the following statements as True or False, according to the meaning of the italicized words.

28. _____ Someone who *carjacks* your car helps you change a tire.

29. _____ The *gentrification* of a neighborhood is of particular benefit to the poor, who would find it difficult to relocate otherwise.

30. _____ *Infomercials* can be misleading to the public, who may be under the impression that the program is centered on news and information.

ANSWERS

Here are some clues to the meanings of some words in this lesson:

 Glitterati looks like *glitter.*

 Micromanage contains *micro-*, which means "small."

 Flextime looks like *flexible.*

 Multimedia begins with *multi-*, which means "many."

Now see how you did at filling in the sources of words in the table on the next page.

Word List 17: Answer Table

Words	Possible Sources
infomercial	a blend of *information* and *commerical*
emoticon	a combination of *emotion* and *icon*
LIFO	acronym for "*l*ast *i*n, *f*irst *o*ut"
carjack	a combination of *car* and *jack*
glitterati	a blend of *glitter* and *literature* (literati)
cords	shortening of *corduroys*
fax	a shortening of *facsimile*
micromanage	a combination of *micro-* ("small") and *manage*
emcee	from the initials "M" and "C" in *Master of Ceremonies*
docudrama	a blend of *documentary* and *drama*
telecommuter	a blend of *telecommunications* and *commuter*
perk	a shortening of *prerequisite*
flextime	from *flexible* and *time*
multimedia	a blend of *multi-* ("many") and *media*
gentrification	a word coined from *gentry* ("upper class")

A Closer Look

Shortenings

1. fan
2. condo
3. flu
4. dorm
5. deli

Acronyms

6. LIFO
7. UNICEF
8. WYSIWIG
9. CORE
10. NATO
11. MADD
12. yuppies

Blends

13. dancercise
14. astronaut
15. sitcom
16. multiplex
17. telethon

Words from Proper Names

18. Scotch
19. Jello
20. Band-aids
21. Xerox
22. thermos

Practice Exercises

Fill in the Blanks

23. micromanage
24. emoticons
25. docudrama
26. telecommuters
27. flextime

True or False?

28. False
29. False
30. True

IN SHORT

In this lesson, you have looked at how new words enter the language from often various sources—popular culture, industry trends, and technological innovations, among others. It is a mark of the flexibility and beauty of English that it can expand in such interesting ways.

LESSON

18

CAMPUS-SPEAK

In this lesson, you will meet words that you would encounter on a college campus or in any post–high-school academic program. Whether or not college is in your future, the words in this lesson are good to know. You'll come across them in newspapers and magazines, on the radio, and even on television at one time or another.

If you're planning to attend college classes or have a son, daughter, or spouse who is, you'll want to be familiar with the words in this lesson. They're part of any educated person's general vocabulary. In earlier lessons, you've already met two words that are heard frequently around the campus:

- *tenure:* protected employment for professors who have reached a certain level of rank or experience. A related term is *tenure track,* which means that a position carries with it the possibility of tenure.
- *prerequisite:* requirements needed before a promotion or the granting of a job. In college, the word (sometimes shortened to *prereq*) refers to the course or courses that you must take in order to qualify for an advanced course.

In this lesson, you'll be introduced to 15 other words that are part of the world of *academia*, or the world of education.

WORD LIST 18

What follows are some other often-used words on the campus. See how many are familiar to you. As before:

- Read all the sentences.
- Underline bold words you already know and can define by sight.
- Put a star over bold words that seem familiar but that you cannot define by sight.
- Circle words in bold that are unfamiliar to you.

Sentences

syllabus

practicum

transcript

sabbatical

The news around campus was that my school was going to adopt the **semester** system in place of the existing **trimester** system.

The **bursar's** office required that the **tuition** check be notarized.

My **syllabus,** or course outline, said that there would be midterm and final exams in the course, as well as a required **practicum.**

The **alumni** raised funds for the new **dormitory.**

The **registrar** sent my **transcript** to the list of people I gave her.

I was disappointed that the famous professor whose class I took was on **sabbatical** leave that semester.

The core **curriculum** in my school was weighted toward the **liberal arts** but allowed for a number of **electives** in the sciences.

The requirements for a **master's degree** included six **credits** of math.

Fill in the rest of the table on the next page according to your understanding of this lesson's words from these sentences.

Word List 18: Practice Table

Word	Syllables	Possible Meaning
semester	se-mes-ter	one of two parts of the academic year
bursar	bur-sar	treasurer
tuition	tu-i-tion	payment for courses
syllabus	syl-la-bus	class outline
practicum		
alumni		
dormitory		
registrar		
transcript		
sabbatical		
core curriculum		
liberal arts		
elective		
master's degree		
credit		

A CLOSER LOOK
Latin Origins

You will notice that many words related to academic life are derived from Latin. This is because when the university system originated in the Middle Ages, all teaching was carried on in Latin. The word *campus* itself comes from a Latin word meaning "a plain or a gathering place." Other Latin words in this lesson include:

- *curriculum*, from the Latin root *curr*, meaning "to run." A *curriculum* is a "running" through a body of knowledge. The word *course* is also derived from this root.
- *dormitory*, from the Latin *dor*, which means "to sleep."
- *credit*, from the Latin root *cred*, meaning "to believe." When you have earned credits, it is believed that you have mastered the material in the course.
- *alumni*, the plural form of the Latin word *alumnus* (feminine form *alumna*), which meant "a foster son or daughter."
- *bursar*, from the Latin *burs*, meaning "purse." Remember from Lesson 7 that *reimbursement* means "a return of payment." And *disbursements* are payments from funds in hand (or purse).
- *elective* contains the Latin *e(x)* ("out of") and *legere* ("to choose").

Roots and Prefixes

Match the italicized word parts in column A with their meanings in column B.

A	B
1. _____ *sem*ester	**a.** a written record
2. _____ *dor*mitory	**b.** a two-term year
3. _____ *cred*its	**c.** units believed to be completed
4. _____ tran*script*	**d.** a place to sleep

Find the Word

Circle the word from this lesson in each group:

5. purser / bursar / bursitis / burst / pursed / burner / burnish

6. practical / practitioner / practicum / practical / practice / premium

7. register / registration / registrar / regulation / regimen / regency

8. seminar / seminole / semmester / semesster / semester

9. credible / credence / credit / creed / creditable / credulous

Meanings for Word List 18

You've been given clues to these words in the sentences and Latin origins. How many did you know?

semester (SUH-mes-ter): one of two terms in an academic year

bursar (BUR-sahr): the financial officer of a college

tuition (too-ISH-uhn): payment for course work

syllabus (SIL-ah-bus): the course requirements for a particular course

practicum (PRAK-ti-kum): a part of a course in which a student works on a related project outside the classroom

alumni (a-LUM-nye): graduates of a particular institution

dormitory (DOR-mi-tor-ee): a residence for students who live on campus

registrar (REJ-is-trahr): the person or office charged with the record keeping at a school or college

transcript (TRAN-skript): an official copy of a student's school record.

sabbatical (suh-BAT-i-kuhl): a leave permitted for teachers to pursue advanced study, travel, or opportunities for professional development

core curriculum (KOHR ku-RIK-yoo-luhm): a series of courses required of all students in a particular school or school program

liberal arts (li-ber-uhl ARTZ): academic disciplines that provide information of general cultural concern

elective (e-LEK-tiv): course chosen by the student

master's degree (MAS-terz duh-gree): an academic degree at least one year beyond a bachelor's degree

credit (KRED-it): completed unit of study in school

PRACTICE EXERCISES

Test your knowledge of the words in this lesson by completing the following exercises.

Unscramble

Find the word from Word List 18 in the scrambled words.

10. restargir _____

11. rotyromid _____

12. laslubys _____

13. lacitbabas _____

14. strintprac _____

15. mulain _____

Fill in the Blanks

Complete the spelling of the following:

16. sc__ __ __ter

17. li__ __ __ __l arts

18. pra__ __ __ __um

19. tui__ __ __ __

20. mas__ __ __'s

True or False?

Mark the following sentences as True or False, according to the meaning of the highlighted word or phrase:

21. _____ You can pursue your *master's degree* only after you have earned your bachelor's degree.

22. _____ A *core curriculum* is made up of electives.

23. _____ Students get a *sabbatical* when they don't have to go to class on Sundays.

24. _____ A *practicum* is a course in which the student is involved with activities outside the classroom that are still related to course content.

25. _____ Your *transcript* would show how many credits you had earned in the humanities.

ANSWERS

Using word meaning strategies, you can see these clues in some of this lesson's words:

Syllabus is unlikely to look familiar. You need a context to get the meaning of this word.

Practicum has the word *practice* in it.

Transcript contains the prefix *trans-*, which means "across" and the root *scrip*, which means "to write." A *transcript* is a "writing across" of your school record.

Sabbatical has the word *sabbath* in it, which means "day of rest." A *sabbatical* leave is meant to be a period of rest and renewal.

Does your completed table look similar to the one on the next page?

Word List 18: Answer Table

Word	Syllables	Possible Meaning
semester	se-mes-ter	one of two parts of the academic year
bursar	bur-sar	treasurer
tuition	tu-i-tion	payment for courses
syllabus	syl-la-bus	class outline
practicum	prac-ti-cum	a session for getting practical experience in a field
alumni	a-lum-ni	graduates
dormitory	dor-mi-tor-y	where students sleep
registrar	reg-is-trar	the person who registers you for courses
transcript	tran-script	an academic record
sabbatical	sab-bat-i-cal	a temporary leave
core curriculum	core cur-ric-u-lum	the courses around which the curriculum is built
liberal arts	li-ber-al arts	courses in art and literature
elective	e-lec-tive	a course the student can choose
master's degree	mas-ter's de-gree	an academic degree at least one year beyond a bachelor's
credit	cred-it	unit or "hour" earned for completing course work

A Closer Look

Roots and Prefixes

1. b
2. d
3. c
4. a

Find the Word

5. bursar
6. practicum
7. registrar
8. semester
9. credit

Practice Exercises

Unscramble

10. registrar
11. dormitory
12. syllabus
13. sabbatical
14. transcript
15. alumni

True or False?

21. True
22. False
23. False
24. True
25. True

Fill in the Blanks

16. se*mes*ter
17. li*beral* arts
18. pra*ctic*um
19. tui*tion*
20. mas*ter*'s

IN SHORT

In this lesson, you became acquainted with some of the vocabulary you would hear around a college campus or find in a college publication. It is helpful to know these terms if you are a full-time or part-time college student or are in the process of returning to school or choosing a college for yourself or a family member. Moreover, many of these words are considered part of an educated person's general vocabulary.

LESSON 19

LOOKING BACKWARD

Here's your chance to really test yourself. See how well you can use the clues from the four strategies to word meaning—sight, sound, structure, and context—to recognize and define words taken from each of the lessons in the book.

If you have been working sequentially through this book, you've added well over 100 words to your reading vocabulary—perhaps as many as 30 or more in a single week. And you've learned four strategies for figuring out the meanings of words when you meet them in print.

The point of learning those techniques, however, is not just to help you learn only the words in this book, but also to give you the means for learning an equal or greater number of words every week of your life, for the *rest of your life*.

In this lesson, you will return one more time to the words you've encountered so far in these pages. You'll follow the four approaches to word meaning, but this time, the words in each section will be drawn from the entire book. If you don't recognize or remember a word, you can turn to the Appendix, where you'll find an alphabetical list of the words and the lessons in which each can be found.

Here's what to do:

- Do as many of the exercises as you can in each section.
- Check your answers against the answer key at the end of the lesson.
- Circle those words you have forgotten or want to review.
- Look up the lesson number in the Appendix.
- Find the words you have forgotten and take another look at them.
- Be patient; it takes a while to get good at this!

STRATEGY 1: MEANING FROM SIGHT

In Lessons 1 and 2, you learned ways to recognize words by the way they look. See how many of them below you recognize by sight.

A Word in a Crowd

Circle the word from the previous 18 lessons in each of the following groups of words.

1. executive / execrable / executor / execute / excrete / exit
2. barrier / baritone / buried / barricade / barrio / bard / barred
3. wholistic / holy / hostility / holistic / wholesome / holiday
4. infest / manifest / infestation / manifestation
5. merger / merchandise / merganser / merge / management

Split Personalities

Each of the words in the word bank is a homograph or homonym. Match each with its multiple meanings.

Word Bank:

> **a.** icon   **b.** contract   **c.** monitor   **d.** cameo
>
> **e.** seasoned   **f.** cloning   **g.** mouse

6. _____ a religious image
7. _____ to enter into a legal agreement
8. _____ a small, often uncredited role in a movie
9. _____ a popular, highly influential person
10. _____ experienced
11. _____ a pointing device on a computer
12. _____ to observe the activities of a person or group of people
13. _____ to become smaller
14. _____ a kind of jewelry made with a carved image on top of a stone base

15. _____ a small domestic rodent

16. _____ asexual reproduction

17. _____ making exact copies of computer components

18. _____ flavored

19. _____ a small image on a computer screen that signals a program or operation on the computer

20. _____ a computer screen

Home Base

How many "family members" can you name from the following base words? Try to name one for each part of speech indicated. Be sure to include at least one word from the previous lessons on each line.

21. feminine (verb) _____

(noun)_____

22. immune (verb) _____

(noun)_____

23. tranquil (verb) _____

(noun)_____

24. profit (noun) _____

(adjective)_____

25. elect (noun) _____

(adjective)_____

STRATEGY 2: MEANING FROM SOUND

In Lesson 4, you learned how to sound out words to detect meaning. See how many you can sound out from the words you've learned.

Phonics Is "Phundamental"!

1. Circle the words in which the letter *g* carries the sound of *j*.

rigid / trilogy / genome / ghetto / digital / gestation / morgue / merger / prognosis

2. Circle the words in which the letter *c* carries the sound of *s*.

emcee / cynicism / draconian / cartel / recession / cinema / capital / narcissist / coroner / caveat / recipient / critic

3. The letter *c* sounds like *s*, and the letter *g* sounds like *j*, when the *c* and *g* are followed by the letter _____, _____, or _____.

Divide and Conquer

Divide the following words into syllables according to the rules you learned in
Lesson 4.

4. hiatus _____

5. improvisation _____

6. revival _____

7. surrogate _____

8. arbitration_____

9. tycoon _____

10. recession _____

11. laconic _____

12. entitlement _____

A Two-for-One: Synonyms and Antonyms

Draw a line between each word in column A and its *synonym* (word that means
the same) in column B.

A	B
13. neonatal	**a.** host
14. trauma	**b.** shock
15. coalition	**c.** graduates
16. alumni	**d.** newborn
17. emcee	**e.** alliance

Draw a line between each word in column A and its *antonym* (word that means
the opposite) in column B.

A	B
18. seasoned	**a.** colleagues
19. commendations	**b.** genuine
20. ersatz	**c.** prerequisite
21. elective	**d.** inexperienced
22. opponents	**e.** criticisms

STRATEGY 3: MEANING FROM STRUCTURE

In Lessons 5–12, you learned how to recognize those parts of a word that give a clue to its meaning. See how well you use structural clues to recognize and recall the words you've learned.

Your Roots Are Showing

Mark the following statements as True or False, according to the meaning suggested by the italicized root in the word.

1. _____ You would need a *venti*lator to assist your hearing.

2. _____ You could vote by *proxy* only if you were present.

3. _____ *Hydra*ulic works use water for power.

4. _____ An *archae*ologist is interested in ancient artifacts.

5. _____ *Toxi*cology is the study of plant life.

Prefixes: Directional Signals

Prefixes come at the beginning of a word and often change its direction.

Draw a line between the prefixes in column A and their meanings in column B.

A	B
6. *multi-*	**a.** with or together
7. *pre-*	**b.** back or again
8. *re-*	**c.** three
9. *sub-*	**d.** many
10. *com-*	**e.** before
11. *tri-*	**f.** under

Suffixes: Just Playing a Part

Suffixes come at the end of a word and tell the reader what role the word is playing in that particular sentence. At different times, words act as nouns, verbs, adjectives, or adverbs. In the following sentences, circle the word that tells what part each of the highlighted suffixes is playing in the sentence.

12. We often look to government funding to subsid*ize* the arts.

noun / verb / adjective / adverb

13. In a reces*sion*, jobs are often scarce and money is tight.

noun / verb / adjective / adverb

14. The artist had a retrospec*tive* exhibition of his work.

noun / verb / adjective / adverb

15. Hol*istic* medicine aims to treat the whole person, not just the symptoms of the illness.

noun / verb / adjective / adverb

16. Louis Pasteur discovered how to pasteur*ize* milk.

noun / verb / adjective / adverb

17. She behaved negligent*ly* when she failed to put seat belts on her children.

noun / verb / adjective / adverb

"Put It All Together, and It Spells. . . "

A good eye for the meanings suggested by parts of a word can lead you to a good ear for the meanings of whole words. In the following sentences, fill in the missing part of the word.

18. A play that is presented some time after its original production is a

__ __vival.

19. A performance that is unrehearsed is an improvisa__ __ __ __.

20. A two-party political system is a __ __partisan system.

21. A neo__ __ __ologist works with newborns in the hospital.

22. A _ _ _ motion is when someone is raised to a higher position or rank.

23. An equivalent or a return for something done or given is called a

re _ _ _ _ _ _ _ _.

24. Someone who is traveling __ __cognito might use a false name or

pseudo__ __ __.

Just for Fun: Making Them Up

A good way to test your recognition of significant word parts is to "translate" non-sense words into something that could be a real word. Match the nonsense words in column A and their possible meanings in column B.

A	B
25. retoxicate	**a.** bad breath
26. multimetrical	**b.** of two feelings
27. dormicide	**c.** newly changeable
28. subcision	**d.** many measured
29. bipathic	**e.** sleep killing
30. neomutable	**f.** a cut from underneath
31. malspiration	**g.** poison again

32. Now, go one step more and divide the nonsense words into syllables to

test your skill. _____,

_____, _____,

_____, _____,

_____, and _____.

STRATEGY 4: WORD MEANING FROM CONTEXT

In Lessons 13 and 14, you learned how to determine word meaning from the context of the sentence or paragraph in which the word appears. The specific ways you learned to determine meaning from context are by means of context clues. The clues you learned were:

Definition   Example   Contrast   Restatement

Clueless? Don't Be!

Identify the kind of context clue that is offered in the following sentences for each word.

1. Though he liked the flexibility of *per diem* work, she preferred the security of regular, full-time employment. Context clue by

_____.

2. She pursued a career as an *audiologist* because she was anxious to help people with hearing problems. Context clue by

_____.

3. He was so *narcissistic* that he couldn't pass a mirror without taking a look at himself. Context clue by _____.

4. *Docudramas*, which approach documentary subjects in a dramatic way, are popular forms of entertainment. Context clue by

_____.

5. The students received a *syllabus* at the beginning of the course. This course outline contained all the dates for exams and term papers for the semester. Context clue by _____.

6. Despite the comments by political *pundits* that the welfare reform bill was doomed, the legislature instead listened to the wishes of average constituents who claimed no special expertise. Context clue by

_____.

7. His *stoicism* was well known. He worked without complaint even when suffering the side effects of chemotherapy. Context clue by

_____.

8. In the seventeenth century, the *bourgeois*, or middle class, opposed the privileges held by nobles. Context clue by _____.

9. The *maverick* politician refused to follow his party's lead, which made him an outcast in the legislature. Context clue by _____.

Attention, Please!

See if you can use the context clues in the following sentences to determine the missing word in each one.

10. They believed that they could have a relationship that was _____, that is, did not include a physical attraction.

11. By gaining sole control of the major share of the markets, the computer company had a virtual _____ in the industry.

12. _____ can be very addictive. That's why it is so hard to quit smoking.

13. The amputee wore a _____, or artificial replacement, for his missing leg.

14. He enjoyed a good _____, or close communication, with the students in his class.

15. She made a _____ when she brought a glazed ham to her prospective in-laws. How was she to know that the whole family was vegetarian?

16. He received many _____ for his long career in the theater. His shelf full of Oscars, Tony awards, and other honors showed how greatly his work was valued by his peers.

17. Political _____, that is, a performance that pokes fun at political institutions and politicians, is a popular form of television entertainment.

18. Freshman legislators often challenge the leadership of those who are _____, or already in office.

19. The immigration office said that it would _____ her application for a visa. However, it was a long time before the document arrived.

The Familiar and the New

In this book, you also learned a number of words and phrases that were new constructions or common expressions in the language. See how closely you noticed the familiar faces and the new ones.

Idiom's Delight

Complete the familiar expression that belongs in each sentence.

1. I go to the movies rarely, but *once in a* _____, I like to see a Western on the big screen.

2. The new baby was the _____ *image* of her father.

3. It's important to stay calm and not *fly off the* _____ when you hear bad news.

4. Although she was deeply hurt by the criticism, she decided to _____ *off* their remarks.

5. The young politician debated about running for the Senate and finally decided to *take a* _____ at the job.

Blends Are Trends

Fill in the blends made from these word pairs:

6. flexible + time = _____.

7. information + commercial = _____.

8. modulating + demodulating = _____.

9. car + hijack = _____.

10. microscopic + management = _____.

11. medical + care = _____.

And in Passing . . .

There were a number of words or terms that were introduced throughout the book that were not on the word lists themselves. See how many you remember from your trip through the text.

Word Bank

a. acronym **e.** connotation **i.** eponyms
b. phonics **f.** neologisms **j.** homograph
c. syllables **g.** schwa **k.** homonyms
d. denotation **h.** cliché **l.** colloquialisms

1. An expression that is outworn and stale is a(n) _____.

2. The system of letter sounds and symbols is _____.

3. The associated meaning of a word is its _____.

4. Words based on proper names are _____.

5. The *uh* sound in a word is shown in the dictionary by _____.

6. Words that sound alike and are sometimes spelled alike but have different meanings are _____.

7. The literal meaning of a word is its _____.

8. A word made up of the first letters of the words in a name or phrase is called a(n) _____.

9. When a word is divided into its sound bites, each of which contains at least one vowel, it is divided into its _____.

10. New words that enter the language are called _____.

11. Words that are spelled the same but that have different meanings are called _____.

12. Grammatically incorrect but frequently heard expressions are often examples of _____.

ANSWERS

Strategy 1: Meaning from Sight
A Word in a Crowd
1. executor
2. barrio
3. holistic
4. manifest
5. merger

Split Personalities
6. a
7. b
8. d
9. a
10. e
11. g
12. c
13. b
14. d
15. g
16. f
17. f
18. e
19. a
20. c

Home Base
21. feminize, feminist
22. immunize, immunization
23. tranquilize, tranquility
24. profiteer *or* profiteering, profitable
25. election, electoral

Strategy 2: Meaning from Sound

Phonics is "Phundamental"!

1. rigid, trilogy, genome, digital, gestation, merger

2. emcee, cynicism, recession, cinema, narcissist, recipient

3. *e, i,* or *y*

Divide and Conquer	Synonyms and Antonyms
4. hi-a-tus	**13.** d
5. im-prov-i-sa-tion	**14.** b
6. re-viv-al	**15.** e
7. sur-ro-gate	**16.** c
8. ar-bi-tra-tion	**17.** a
9. ty-coon	**18.** d
10. re-ces-sion	**19.** e
11. la-con-ic	**20.** b
12. en-ti-tle-ment	**21.** c
	22. a

Strategy 3: Meaning from Structure

Your Roots Are Showing	Suffixes
1. False	**12.** verb
2. False	**13.** noun
3. True	**14.** adjective
4. True	**15.** adjective
5. False	**16.** verb
	17. adverb

Prefixes

6. d

7. e

8. b

9. f

10. a

11. c

"Put It All Together ..."

18. *re*vival

19. improvisa*tion*

20. *bi*partisan

21. neo*nat*al

22. *pro*motion

23. re*compense*

24. *in*cognito; pseudo*nym*

Making Them Up

25. g

26. d

27. e

28. f

29. b

30. c

31. a

32. re-tox-i-cate, mul-ti-met-ri-cal, dor-mi-cide, sub-ci-sion, bi-path-ic, ne-o-mu-ta-ble, *and* mal-spir-a-tion

Strategy 4: Meaning from Context

Clueless? Don't Be!

1. contrast

2. definition

3. example

4. definition

5. restatement

6. contrast

7. example

8. definition

9. example; definition

Attention, Please!

10. platonic

11. monopoly

12. nicotine

13. prosthesis

14. rapport

15. faux pas

16. kudos *or* commendations

17. satire

18. incumbent

19. expedite

The Familiar and the New

Idiom's Delight

1. blue moon

2. spitting

3. handle

4. laugh

5. stab

Blends Are Trends

6. flextime

7. infomercial

8. modem

9. carjack

10. micromanage

11. Medicare

And in Passing . . .

1. h
2. b
3. e
4. i
5. g
6. k

7. d
8. a
9. c
10. f
11. j
12. l

LESSON

20

LOOKING FORWARD

This final lesson gives you one last chance to test your ability to apply the four approaches to the meaning of words. The three passages in this lesson represent the kinds of writing you come across in real life. See how well you can determine the meaning of words in them that you have not seen, using all that you've learned in this book.

Here, in the last few pages of this book, you'll test your wings, so to speak, in three readings—passages that could very well be articles in magazines or newspapers you see every day. Words in each passage are singled out for you. As you consider them, remember that you've got four ways to approach each word, and any one of them could unlock the meaning for you:

- "Does it look like anything I've ever seen?"
- "Does it sound like anything I've ever heard?"
- "Does any part of the word give me a hint?"
- "Does the rest of the sentence or paragraph give me a clue?"

Keep in mind as you go along that you're drawing from your own background and experiences as a reader and a speaker. You may respond to a visual clue in a word, or you might instead hear a familiar sound in that word. Or perhaps you'll associate a prefix you see with the same prefix on another word you know already. The point is that *you have resources in your own language store that will help you recognize the meanings of unfamiliar words.* Once you develop those resources and get in the habit of using them, the world of words opens up to you as never before.

Here's what to do:

- Read the passages.
- Note the italicized words.
- Answer the questions that follow.
- Check your answers against the answer key near the end of this lesson.

PASSAGE 1: A BUSINESS COMMENTARY
Superstores: Coming to a Neighborhood Near You!

In urban neighborhoods around the country, neighborhood shop owners watch in *consternation* as blocks of empty warehouses are replaced by warehouse-style retail stores. These so-called "superstores" generally carry low-end merchandise at discount prices and offer customers the convenience of shopping carts and free parking as *incentives* for buying in volume.

Supporters of the superstore owners and investors point to the fact that by making good commercial use of abandoned or underused property, they are fighting the ugly effects of urban *blight*. In addition, they maintain that the large size of these stores enables them to employ large numbers of community residents and thus enhance their buying power for other businesses in the area.

Owners of local *bodegas*, mom and pop shops and other small businesses, however, are outraged at what they regard as unfair competition by the big stores. They say that they can't compete with the corporate buying power of the big store owners, that they can't stock such a large variety of items or offer the same low prices. They say that increased car and truck traffic in the local streets is dangerous and unhealthy. They also lose their daily "foot traffic" because neighborhood shoppers now wait until the weekend to hitch a ride and *stock up* at the superstore.

Customers, for their part, are often *ambivalent* about the big stores. Although they appreciate the convenience and lower prices, they are aware that when they ignore the local small shop owner, they are ignoring a neighbor who may speak their language, give them credit in tough times, and be part of the larger *ethnic* community. They are unhappy when they see the effect of a business downturn on the families of the shop owners who are their friends. Many feel that the character of a community is reflected in its commerce and that shuttered shops are often the first step to shattered neighborhoods.

1. From the context clue by example, the word *consternation* is most likely to mean
   a. joy.
   b. painful confusion.
   c. anticipation.

2. From the context clue by example, the word *incentive* is most likely to mean
   a. encouragement.
   b. discouragement.
   c. deterrent.

3. From the context clue by definition, the word *blight* is most likely to mean
   a. development.
   b. ugliness.
   c. budget cuts.

4. The appearance of the word *bodega* suggests that the word means
   a. department store.
   b. repair shop.
   c. Spanish grocery store.

5. Given the prefix *ambi-*, the word *ambivalent* most likely means
   a. of two minds.
   b. opinionated.
   c. opposed.

6. From the sound of the word *ethnic*, its most likely meaning is
   a. language group.
   b. interest group.
   c. political group.

7. From the context of the sentence, the idiom *stock up* is most likely to mean
   a. buy very little.
   b. buy a lot.
   c. pay higher prices.

PASSAGE 2: FROM A JOURNAL OF EDUCATION
The Kitchen Table Classroom

For an increasing number of school-age children, the little red school house is home sweet home. Homeschooling is one of the fastest-growing trends in American education, as thousands of parents *eschew* both public and private school options and instead teach their children at home. Once largely the province of religious families who feared the *secular* influence of public education, homeschoolers now draw from a broad spectrum of social, economic, and religious groups.

Proponents of homeschooling point out that children schooled at home are not limited to the demands or time frames of a school curriculum but can work at their own pace for as long as is needed to master a skill. They assert that homeschooling can be more flexible and allow for greater creativity on the part of the learners. They note that homeschooled children are held to the same standards of achievement as traditionally schooled children and that on *mandated* tests required by the state, their performance is, on average, equal to or superior to public school students.

Mainstream educators acknowledge that surveys do show that homeschoolers in many ways appear to learn at home as well as they do in school. They argue, however, that although homeschoolers can certainly have social interactions with other children in after-school settings such as sports, music, clubs, and other activities, they miss out on the *diversity* of the various social contacts that are part of the classroom setting. They note as well that some parents lack the expertise that allows them to add information beyond the textbook lessons, especially in the areas of math and science.

Indeed, it is because of the limitations of homeschooling's access to laboratories and upper-level math instruction that the majority of homeschoolers over the years have chosen to end their homeschooling by eighth or ninth grade. In recent years, however, cooperative colleges and high schools have allowed some homeschoolers to take specialized courses as *externs*. Increasing, too, are the opportunities for students to take distance-learning courses through the Internet. In fact, the computer may be the single greatest *facilitator* of homeschooling to emerge in the past ten years. Most homeschoolers will say that homeschooling is not for everyone. But in the menu of educational choices open to American families, it is an increasingly popular option.

8. From the context clue by example, the most likely meaning of *eschew* is

   a. enhance.

   b. avoid.

   c. disrespect.

9. From the contrast clue in the sentence, the most likely meaning of the word *secular* is

   a. worldly.

   b. frightening.

   c. unfamiliar.

10. The prefix *pro-* in the word *proponents* suggests that the word means

   a. enemies.

   b. supporters.

   c. practitioners.

11. The context clue by restatement suggests that the word *mandated* means

   a. neglected.

   b. outdated.

   c. required.

12. The word *diversity* looks like the word *diverse*, which suggests that *diversity* means

   a. uniformity.

   b. disadvantages.

   c. variety.

13. The prefix *ex-* gives a structural clue to the word *extern*, which most likely means

   a. employees.

   b. inside staff.

   c. people from outside the workplace or school.

14. The word *facilitator* sounds like the word *facilitate*, which suggests that *facilitator* means

   a. an enabler.

   b. an enemy.

   c. an outcast.

PASSAGE 3: A POLITICAL ANALYSIS
Liberty's Lamp: Still Held High

When the Statue of Liberty was rededicated in 1985, it was amid great fanfare and attention, which focused largely on the traditional role of the United States as a beacon of hope for the *disenfranchised* and dispossessed peoples of the world. That beacon has flickered rather dimly in recent years, *buffeted* by winds of discontent, as Americans have reassessed their commitment to that American ideal of equal opportunity and hope for all who reach our shores.

The last decade has seen evidence of growing concern with two major issues related to immigration. The first is the issue of labor competition. During what is generally *conceded* to be a period of decline in the power of organized labor, there has been widening discontent over the *influx* of unskilled workers from Mexico, the Caribbean, and third-world countries, who will work for low wages and few, if any, benefits. Those benefits are the source of the second significant immigration issue that has received much debate and *speculation* at local, state, and national levels.

Communities that have large immigrant populations complain that their resources are strained to the breaking point by the costs of housing, education, and healthcare for large numbers of both legal and illegal *aliens*. Congress has made numerous and largely unsatisfactory efforts to balance the interests of communities with the real human needs of people new to this country. There have been calls for tightening the net against illegal residents and restricting the numbers of immigrants in general.

Despite these concerns, however, there are those who point out that the contributions of newcomers to our communities far outweigh their costs. They bring energy and entrepreneurship in the establishment of new businesses and a healthy competition in the workplace. Most immigrant groups value education as a means to success and contribute to the *revitalization* of public schools and community resources.

Ethnic diversity enriches the cultural fabric of our society. As the new *millenium* begins, then, we might hope that the Lady in the Harbor will soon survey a new era of cooperation and compassion among all who call themselves Americans.

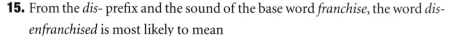

15. From the *dis-* prefix and the sound of the base word *franchise*, the word *disenfranchised* is most likely to mean

   a. not allowed to vote.

   b. not allowed to eat.

   c. fortunate.

16. From the context clue by example, the word *buffeted* is most likely to mean
   a. challenged.
   b. battered.
   c. confirmed.

17. From the prefix *con-* and the root *cede* ("to give"), the word *conceded* is most likely to mean
   a. denied.
   b. proven.
   c. yielded.

18. From the prefix *in-* and the root *flux* ("to flow"), the word *influx* is most likely to mean
   a. drain.
   b. loss.
   c. addition.

19. The appearance of the word *speculation* suggests that the word means
   a. consideration.
   b. hostility.
   c. dread.

20. From the context clue by example, the word *aliens* most likely means
   a. neighbors.
   b. outsiders.
   c. attorneys.

21. The prefix *re-* and the base word *vital* suggest that the word *revitalization* means
   a. destruction.
   b. rebuilding.
   c. complication.

22. The prefix *mille-* suggests that the word *millenium* most likely means
   a. the end of ten years.
   b. the end of a hundred years.
   c. the end of a thousand years.

ANSWERS

Passage 1	Passage 2	Passage 3
1. b	**8.** b	**15.** a
2. a	**9.** a	**16.** b
3. b	**10.** b	**17.** c
4. c	**11.** c	**18.** c
5. a	**12.** c	**19.** a
6. a	**13.** c	**20.** b
7. b	**14.** a	**21.** b
		22. c

Words to the Wise

If you've taken the time to work through each lesson of the book, you will have not only added 100 or more words to your vocabulary, you'll also have learned some very useful strategies that you can use from now on to figure out hundreds of other new and interesting words. You've become a better reader and speaker of the language, and you've built skills and recognition abilities that will continue to grow with you. Just how much have you grown so far in your "word-ability"? Find out for yourself. The following list of questions should look familiar. It's the same list that you saw way back at the start of this book, on page vii. Read it again and fill in your answers. If you wrote in your answers the first time, compare the two sets. If you didn't answer the questions the first time around, do so now so that you get a sense of how you see yourself as a learner.

Check the sentences that describe your own vocabulary habits:

_____ **1.** I don't feel confident that I express myself well when I speak.

_____ **2.** I sometimes feel uncomfortable when I know what I want to say but just can't think of the right word.

_____ **3.** I notice unfamiliar words in print and feel that I should know them.

_____ **4.** I have trouble remembering words I learned in school.

_____ **5.** If I write down new words, I remember them better.

_____ **6.** Sometimes, I notice that words look and sound like other words.

_____ **7.** If I come across an unfamiliar word in print, I usually look it up in the dictionary.

_____ **8.** If I come across an unfamiliar word in print, I usually ask someone what it means.

_____ **9.** If I hear an unfamiliar word in conversation or on the radio or TV,
I usually ask someone what it means.

_____ **10.** If I meet a word I don't know, I am usually too embarrassed to ask
for help or to look up its meaning.

IN SHORT

As you turn away from this book and turn your eyes and ears toward the
words that fill your life, take pleasure in recognizing the new words you've
learned out there in the world. There's a kind of _gotcha!_ feeling when you see
one of "your" words in a newspaper, a magazine article, or a book. And it's a
thrill to recognize an unusual or sophisticated word because some piece of it
reminded you of another word and you were able to make the connection.
These are good feelings for us all, and they remind us of the genuine enjoy-
ment we can get from the language we share.

POSTTEST

Now that you've spent a good deal of time improving your vocabulary, take this posttest to see how much you've learned. If you took the pretest at the beginning of this book, you have a good way to compare what you knew when you started the book with what you know now.

When you complete this test, grade yourself, and then compare your score with your score on the pretest. If your score now is much greater that your pretest score, congratulations—you've profited noticeably from your hard work. If your score shows little improvement, perhaps there are certain lessons you need to review. Whatever your score on this posttest, keep this book around for a review and to refer to when you are unsure of a specific word or its meaning.

Match each word in column A with its definition in column B.

A

1. satire
2. proxy
3. kinetic
4. merger
5. solstice
6. demoralize
7. lethargic
8. apartheid
9. hydraulic
10. incumbent
11. coroner
12. rapport
13. profiteer
14. hacker
15. recession
16. bursar
17. mandated
18. seasoned
19. hold off
20. commendation
21. emcee
22. elective
23. incentive
24. be a wash

B

a. the individual structure of human genes that carries the characteristic of the organism
b. the state or period of holding a particular job
c. a period of diminished business activity
d. foolishly idealistic
e. one who is currently serving in a political office
f. distrust of the motives of others
g. a social error
h. a person who invades the computer systems of other people, often illegally
i. an authority on something. This word is most often heard with regard to politics.
j. something that commends; an award or other citation
k. pertaining to information used in a court of law
l. a kind of writing that makes fun of institutions, people, or events as a form of criticism
m. the everyday language spoken by people, or the variety of that language spoken by a specific group
n. the ability to bear pain without complaint
o. policy of official separation of the races in South Africa
p. delay
q. related to motion or movement
r. even out
s. sleepy, sluggish
t. a combining of two or more business into one
u. a physician who examines a body after death
v. the renovating of older, often marginal, neighborhoods for sale to wealthier owners

25. genome

26. modem

27. patron

28. gentrification

29. practicum

30. vernacular

31. pundit

32. tenure

33. quixotic

34. stoicism

35. faux pas

36. cynicism

37. tycoon

38. forensic

39. gestation

40. negligence

w. operated by the force of water or some other liquid

x. one who makes money on an unfortunate incident or situation

y. close communication between people

z. a person who has a lot of money and power

aa. a person authorized to act in the place of another

bb. fear of punishment or the expectation of reward that induces action or motivates effort

cc. the master of ceremonies or host of a performance or program;

dd. a device that allows computers to interact with each other through the Internet by means of the telephone wires

ee. to undermine the confidence or morale of

ff. a part of a course in which a student works on a related project outside the classroom

gg. course chosen by the student

hh. the financial officer of a college

ii. required

jj. habitual carelessness or failure to take proper action

kk. one who supports the arts or sponsors creative efforts

ll. the days on which the sun is farthest from the equator

mm. the length of a pregnancy or time spent in the uterus

nn. experienced

ANSWERS

1. l (Lesson 4)

2. aa (Lesson 8)

3. q (Lesson 5)

4. t (Lesson 9)

5. ll (Lesson 6)

6. e (Lesson 10)

7. s (Lesson 11)

8. o (Lesson 13)

9. w (Lesson 6)

10. e (Lesson 1)

11. u (Lesson 7)

12. y (Lesson 14)

13. x (Lesson 2)

14. h (Lesson 15)

15. c (Lesson 10)

16. hh (Lesson 18)

17. ii (Lesson 20)

18. nn (Lesson 1)

19. p (Lesson 16)

20. j (Lesson 4)

21. cc (Lesson 17)

22. gg (Lesson 18)

23. bb (Lesson 20)

24. r (Lesson 16)

25. a (Lesson 5)

26. dd (Lesson 15)

27. kk (Lesson 3)

28. v (Lesson 17)

29. ff (Lesson 18)

30. m (Lesson 3)

31. i (Lesson 13)

32. b (Lesson 9)

33. d (Lesson 11)

34. n (Lesson 12)

35. g (Lesson 14)

36. f (Lesson 12)

37. z (Lesson 4)

38. k (Lesson 8)

39. mm (Lesson 7)

40. jj (Lesson 2)

APPENDIX

MASTER WORD LIST

Every word highlighted in this book is listed in this Appendix. If you want to refresh your knowledge of any of these words, go to the lesson listed next to the word.

Word	Lesson	Word	Lesson
401(k)	9	be a wash	16
academic	12	bedlam	11
access	15	benefits	10
acquittal	2	bipartisan	1
admiral	13	bistro	13
alumni	18	bouquet	14
ambassador	13	bourgeois	9
anthology	4	bowdlerize	12
apartheid	13	bravado	14
arbitration	9	browser	15
archaeologist	6	burnout	16
audiologist	8	bursar	18
barrio	13	by and large	16

Word	Lesson	Word	Lesson
cameo	4	draconian	12
capital	9	ecosystem	5
carcinogen	5	electives	18
carjack	17	e-mail	15
carte blanche	13	emcee	17
cartel	9	emoticon	17
catalyst	5	entitlement	9
caveat	14	entrepreneur	9
celebrity	3	episode	4
cinema	4	ersatz	13
cloning	5	etiology	7
coalition	1	executor	2
commendation	4	expedite	1
compact disc	15	faux pas	14
compensation	10	fax	17
connoisseur	13	fiasco	13
contract	2	flextime	17
convalesce	7	fly off the handle	16
cool his heels	16	forensic	8
cords	17	franchise	9
core curriculum	18	fraternization	1
coroner	7	furor	1
coterie	14	genome	5
coup d'état	14	gentrification	17
credit	18	gestation	7
critic	3	ghetto	13
crossbreed	5	give it a shot	16
cultural	3	give the slip to	16
cynicism	12	glitterati	17
debilitated	7	global warming	5
defendant	1	graffiti	14
demoralize	10	hacker	15
denim	11	harassment	1
détente	13	hardliner	1
digital	5	herculean	11
docudrama	17	hiatus	4
dormant	6	hold off	16
dormitory	18	holistic	5

Word	Lesson	Word	Lesson
hydraulic	6	miniseries	3
hygiene	11	modem	15
icon	15	monitor	15
immune	7	monopoly	10
import	9	morgue	8
improvisation	4	mouse	15
in vitro	5	multicultural	17
incision	8	multimedia	10
incognito	14	mutation	6
incumbent	1	naiveté	13
inflation	2	narcissistic	12
infomercial	17	negligence	2
Internet	15	neonatologist	8
intruder	2	nicotine	11
invertebrates	5	once in a blue moon	16
jovial	11	online	15
kinetic	5	opponent	4
laconic	11	pandemic	7
laugh off	16	parity	2
lethargic	11	pasteurize	12
levy	9	pathogen	6
liberal arts	18	per diem	9
life of the party	16	periodical	2
LIFO	17	perk	17
maelstrom	13	philosopher	6
malady	8	platonic	11
malapropism	11	portfolio	9
manifest	7	practicum	18
mannequin	14	prerequisite	10
martial	11	primate	6
master's	18	profiteer	2
maverick	11	prognosis	8
Medicare	7	promote	10
memoir	3	prosthesis	7
merger	9	proxy	8
mesmerize	12	pseudonym	3
metric	6	pundit	13
micromanage	17	punitive	1

Word	Lesson	Word	Lesson
quarantined	7	tenure	9
quixotic	11	theory	5
rank and file	9	therapeutic	7
rapport	14	toxicology	8
ratings	3	tranquility	2
realist	1	transcript	18
recession	10	trauma	7
recipient	1	triage	7
recompense	7	trilogy	3
registrar	18	tuition	18
retrospective	3	tycoon	4
revival	3	up to the job	16
rhinestone	11	upload	15
sabbatical	18	utopian	12
satire	4	vandalism	12
savvy	13	ventilation	8
seasoned	1	vernacular	3
semester	18	veto	1
silhouette	11	virulent	5
soliloquy	3	voicemail	15
solstice	6	voucher	1
spitting image	16	watch out	16
spreadsheet	15	website	15
stoicism	12		
studio	3		
subsidize	10		
supporter	3		
surrogate	5		
syllabus	18		
symbiotic	6		
tabloid	3		
take a stab at	16		
telecommuter	17		
telemarketing	10		